# EMOTIONAL TRAPS

## FINDING FREEDOM IN EVERYDAY LIFE

### KRISTEN KANSIEWICZ

All stories and case examples contained in this book are fictional representations. All names and case details have been significantly altered to protect the privacy of any individuals upon which the story themes were based.

All websites or resources listed in this book were available at the time of this publication and may be subject to change. The resources are listed as suggestions but do not necessarily represent a full endorsement by the author.

This book is not intended to give or replace medical advice. The information provided should not be used for self-diagnosis. See a medical professional if you believe you are experiencing mental health symptoms.

Unless otherwise indicated, all Scripture quotations are taken from the Holy Bible, New Living Translation, copyright © 1996, 2004, 2007, 2013 by Tyndale House Foundation. Used by permission of Tyndale House Publishers, Inc., Carol Stream, Illinois 60188. All rights reserved.

Cover photo: Lightspring/Shutterstock
Cover design: Heather Cahill

ISBN:  1-497-36766-2
ISBN-13: 978-1-497-36766-1

To East Coast International Church.
I am grateful to be a part of a body that is
honest in the struggle and determined in
the quest for freedom. May we see His
healing hand upon us as we journey
emotionally and spiritually.

# CONTENTS

# ACKNOWLEDGMENTS

Thank you so much to my husband, Joshua, and my children for giving me extra grace to focus a little more on writing and a little less on laundry.

Thank you to Pastor Kurt Lange, whose simple question led to the development of this book. Thank you for your leadership and for trusting me to do what God has called me to do.

To my team of editors—Linda Bennett, Laurie Hurshman, and Bob Leppanen—thank you!!! You have sacrificed hours of your time to help make this book great in every way. You are the best!

A huge thank you to Heather Cahill, my cover designer. Thank you for lending me your expertise and helping to create an eye-catching product.

I am truly blessed by God to serve in His kingdom and am grateful for His investment in me. May I be faithful to the work He has for me.

# INTRODUCTION

"What exactly makes a person emotionally healthy?" This was the question posed to me by my senior pastor that launched the development of this book, and I believe it is a question many Christians are asking today. As churches have become more vocal about the need for counseling, many have begun to make the connection between spiritual growth and emotional health. Books such as *Boundaries* by Cloud & Townsend as well as *Emotionally Healthy Spirituality* by Peter Scazerro are examples of books written to help Christians improve life skills and approach their faith journey with emotional balance.

While there are a variety of Christian books available to offer guidance on specific emotional skills, there has not yet been a book devoted to helping Christians assess their own emotional health. Taking a step back and looking at some key areas in your life can help you see a bigger picture of emotional problems that may be holding you back from spiritual growth.

Let me introduce you to the heart and soul of this book: the TRAPS assessment. The following five areas together provide a concrete picture of what makes up one's emotional health:

**T**HINKING—Are you able to think about your strengths and weaknesses clearly without feeling either prideful or insecure? Do you have a clear sense of how you present yourself to others and how others may see you? Is your understanding and evaluation of events in your life in line with the perspective of mentors or leaders in your life? In this area of emotional health we are looking for self-awareness, insight, and logical, reasonable thinking.

**R**ELATIONSHIPS—Are your relationships moving you forward spiritually and emotionally or dragging you down? Do you interact with others in your life (friends, family, children) in a way that is positive and constructive or are your relationships filled with conflict? Do you have at least 2-3 friends with whom you can share important feelings as well as a larger group or church setting? Here we are looking for a positive and adequate social network as well as identifying your relational patterns and skills.

ADDICTIONS—Do you have anything in your life that you are dependent on besides God? Addictions can be to substances like nicotine, alcohol, caffeine, or drugs as well as to food, sex, gambling, television, the internet, money, etc. You might be tempted to skip over this area if you have not been addicted to drugs, but it is important to look for any area in which you may be dependent.

PAST—For so many of us, our past continues to impact our present-day lives. For some, there is past trauma or abuse that continues to shape how they see themselves and others. For others, their own mistakes of the past fill them with so much guilt and shame that they feel they can never truly accept God's forgiveness and be free. In assessing this area, focus both on past trauma/abuse AND on shame from past sins or mistakes.

SELF-CARE—Sometimes the everyday, mundane routines can be as critical to emotional and spiritual health as any of the other four areas. Habits such as eating well, regular exercise, good sleep patterns, clear task and time management, and even proper money management are essential to a balanced emotional life. How do you handle stress day-to-day?  Do you have positive coping skills like journaling or hobbies? Do you demonstrate a level of self-discipline and a healthy lifestyle?

In Chapter 1 we will look at the need for addressing emotional issues in the process of spiritual growth. I will lay out a biblical framework for emotional health: what does God say about taking care of our emotional lives? What role does this have in the process of becoming more like Christ? Chapters 2-6 will take an in-depth look at each of the areas in the TRAPS assessment, focusing on specific problem areas and red flags. Chapter 7 will offer practical suggestions for moving forward once emotional traps have been identified. The final chapter will address medications, including why they are sometimes necessary and why Christians should not be afraid to take medications when they are needed. In the appendix you will find a 100-question assessment tool that you can use as a starting point for personal reflection.

Perhaps you are still not quite sold on the emotional/spiritual connection. Isn't the Bible all you need to address life's problems? Some Christians have this point of view: emotional problems derive from sin. Symptoms of depression or anxiety are seen as a result of one's own sinful lifestyle and behaviors. While it is true that we live in a sin-filled and cursed world, not all emotional problems stem from a specific sin you have committed. Your emotional life is far more complex than this, and there are often factors out of your control that contribute to emotional health problems. I hope that this book can help you understand the big picture of emotional health and offer some ideas for moving forward one step at a time.

Galatians 5:1 says, "It is for freedom that Christ has set us free. Stand firm, then, and do not let yourselves be burdened again by a yoke of slavery" (NIV). I pray that this book will greatly benefit you and help you move forward emotionally and spiritually so that we all may experience the freedom Christ has for us in our everyday lives.

# 1

## EMOTIONAL HEALTH IN THE DISCIPLESHIP PROCESS

"How's your emotional health?" This is an essential question for the Christian, for when you engage in a spiritual journey to become like Christ, you must seek freedom in every aspect of your life. Where can you see the fruit of the Holy Spirit, and where are the dead branches? Where do you see the same emotional problems come up again and again in your life?

Emotional traps are common because we live in a cursed world. Whether you have been trapped by your own sin, by the sin of another person, by disease, or by systemic injustice, health and growth are possible. If you are not aware of your emotional traps, you are likely to remain stuck and this can prevent spiritual growth as you are held back by negative

patterns. Like a hamster that continuously runs
on its wheel, expending a lot of energy but never
getting anywhere, so too can we tire ourselves
on the same emotional problems without
spiritually growing.

On this journey to become like Jesus, we
must pursue the emotional and spiritual
wholeness. Throughout Jesus' ministry, He made
the sick well, restored the broken, and set people
free. In order to better understand the ways in
which God defines emotional freedom, let's take
a look at each of the five core areas of emotional
health, asking ourselves, "What does the Bible
describe as a picture of health in this area?"

### THINKING

This area of emotional health relates to
understanding ourselves in proper perspective,
demonstrating wisdom and insight, and filling
our minds with truth instead of negative self-
talk. The following are some of the verses that
paint a picture of what healthy thinking looks
like:

*Psalm 49:3*—For my words are wise, and
my thoughts are filled with insight.

*Romans 12:3*—For by the grace given me I
say to every one of you: Do not think of

yourself more highly than you ought, but rather think of yourself with sober judgment, in accordance with the faith God has distributed to each of you (NIV).

*Ephesians 4:17-18*— So I tell you this, and insist on it in the Lord, that you must no longer live as the Gentiles do, in the futility of their thinking. They are darkened in their understanding and separated from the life of God because of the ignorance that is in them due to the hardening of their hearts (NIV).

*Ephesians 4:23-24*—Instead, let the Spirit renew your thoughts and attitudes. Put on your new nature, created to be like God— truly righteous and holy.

*Philippians 2:3*—Don't be selfish; don't try to impress others. Be humble, thinking of others as better than yourselves.

*Philippians 4:8*—And now, dear brothers and sisters, one final thing. Fix your thoughts on what is true, and honorable, and right, and pure, and lovely, and admirable. Think about things that are excellent and worthy of praise.

> *1 Peter 1:13*—So think clearly and exercise self-control. Look forward to the gracious salvation that will come to you when Jesus Christ is revealed to the world.

Take some time right now to pause and re-read those verses. What do these verses say about the thinking of a follower of Christ? For a moment, reflect on your own ways of thinking. Do you see ways in which your own thinking is at times distorted and not in line with these passages? We'll explore this more in Chapter 2.

## RELATIONSHIPS

The Bible is full of commands and wisdom regarding human relationships. Certainly there are far too many to list here, so I've chosen just a few to start your thinking. Keep in mind that we are not only talking about how we treat each other, but also what types of relationships we have. We also want to consider whether or not we have developed a strong Christian support network including at least 1-2 trusting friend relationships and weekly involvement in a church. Here are some key verses for this area:

> *Psalm 1:1*—Oh, the joys of those who do not follow the advice of the wicked, or

stand around with sinners, or join in with mockers.

*Proverbs 26:27* – If you set a trap for others, you will get caught in it yourself. If you roll a boulder down on others, it will crush you instead.

*Proverbs 27:17*—As iron sharpens iron, so a friend sharpens a friend.

*Romans 12:9*—Don't just pretend to love others. Really love them. Hate what is wrong. Hold tightly to what is good.

*Romans 14:17-19*— For the Kingdom of God is not a matter of what we eat or drink, but of living a life of goodness and peace and joy in the Holy Spirit. If you serve Christ with this attitude, you will please God, and others will approve of you, too. So then, let us aim for harmony in the church and try to build each other up.

*Hebrews 10:24-25*—Let us think of ways to motivate one another to acts of love and good works. And let us not neglect our meeting together, as some people do,

but encourage one another, especially
now that the day of his return is drawing
near.

Pause for a minute to think about the
dynamics of your relationships. Do these verses
on relationships reflect the way you are living
your life? What are some traps that stick out in
your mind? In Chapter 3 we will go much deeper
into this area of relationships.

**ADDICTIONS**

When I think about the life of Christ, I am
reminded of His clear dependence on His Father.
Throughout His ministry, He rejected fame,
money, and the things of this world. Addictions
and dependencies prevent us from complete and
total dependence on God. Some of those
addictions may be life-controlling, and some may
be so subtle you are unaware of how much
control earthly things have in your life. The Bible
is clear that we are to depend on God alone to
supply our every need and we are to avoid
overindulgence of many kinds. Here are a few
verses to spark your thinking on this topic:

*Proverbs 23:29-35*—Who has anguish?
Who has sorrow? Who is always fighting?
Who is always complaining? Who has

unnecessary bruises? Who has bloodshot eyes? It is the one who spends long hours in the taverns, trying out new drinks... And you will say, "They hit me, but I didn't feel it. I didn't even know it when they beat me up. When will I wake up so I can look for another drink?"

*Proverbs 23: 19-21—* My child, listen and be wise: Keep your heart on the right course. Do not carouse with drunkards or feast with gluttons, for they are on their way to poverty, and too much sleep clothes them in rags.

*Proverbs 25:16—* Do you like honey? Don't eat too much, or it will make you sick!

*Ecclesiastes 5:10—*Those who love money will never have enough. How meaningless to think that wealth brings true happiness!

*Matthew 6:24—*No one can serve two masters. For you will hate one and love the other; you will be devoted to one and despise the other. You cannot serve both God and money.

*Ephesians 5:18*—Don't be drunk with wine, because that will ruin your life. Instead, be filled with the Holy Spirit.

*1 Timothy 6:17*—Teach those who are rich in this world not to be proud and not to trust in their money, which is so unreliable. Their trust should be in God, who richly gives us all we need for our enjoyment.

*Hebrews 13:5*—Don't love money; be satisfied with what you have. For God has said, "I will never fail you. I will never abandon you."

When you think of your patterns of behavior, do any addictions come to mind? Most people are comfortable talking about substance addictions, but what about addictions to TV, pornography, or even junk food? Have you ever faced some of these hidden addictions in your own life? Chapter 4 will explore the various areas of addiction more fully.

**PAST**

So many walk around with deep wounds from the past—secrets that they hope no one ever finds out. These issues are usually very difficult to talk about, and many avoid allowing pain from their past to come to the surface. God's word has much to say about a person's past, including these verses specific to those who have experienced abuse or trauma:

> *Psalm 10:18*—You will bring justice to the orphans and the oppressed, so mere people can no longer terrify them.

> *Psalm 71:20*—You have allowed me to suffer much hardship, but you will restore me to life again and lift me up from the depths of the earth.

> *Psalm 75:2*—God says, "At the time I have planned, I will bring justice against the wicked."

> *Psalm 103:6*—The LORD gives righteousness and justice to all who are treated unfairly.

> *Psalm 146:7*—He gives justice to the oppressed and food to the hungry. The LORD frees the prisoners.

> *Isaiah 11:4*—He will give justice to the

poor and make fair decisions for the exploited. The earth will shake at the force of his word, and one breath from his mouth will destroy the wicked.

*2 Corinthians 5:17*—This means that anyone who belongs to Christ has become a new person. The old life is gone; a new life has begun!

These next few verses specifically relate to shame from past mistakes:

*2 Corinthians 7:10* – For the kind of sorrow God wants us to experience leads us away from sin and results in salvation. There's no regret for that kind of sorrow. But worldly sorrow, which lacks repentance, results in spiritual death.

*1 John 3:19-21*— Our actions will show that we belong to the truth, so we will be confident when we stand before God. Even if we feel guilty, God is greater than our feelings, and he knows everything. Dear friends, if we don't feel guilty, we can come to God with bold confidence.

*Romans 5:16*—And the result of God's

gracious gift is very different from the result of that one man's sin. For Adam's sin led to condemnation, but God's free gift leads to our being made right with God, even though we are guilty of many sins.

As you re-read these verses, think of your own past. Are you struggling with past abuse or your own past sins? What might be blocking you from receiving and understanding God's forgiveness? Chapter 5 can help you identify specific emotional traps tied to your past.

## SELF-CARE

Most Christians have some ideas about taking care of their spiritual life. Go to church, read the Bible, pray—these habits are important spiritual disciplines to keep you on track. But many people overlook the connection between the physical care of the body and spiritual health. What difference does it make to my spiritual life if I get enough sleep, exercise, or eat well? Yes, these are healthy habits that a doctor may recommend, but what do they have to do with your spiritual journey? Below are some of God's words about taking care of your body and managing your life with balance:

*3 John 1:2*— Dear friend, I hope all is well with you and that you are as healthy in body as you are strong in spirit.

*Ecclesiastes 11:9-10*— Young people, it's wonderful to be young! Enjoy every minute of it. Do everything you want to do; take it all in. But remember that you must give an account to God for everything you do. So refuse to worry, and keep your body healthy. But remember that youth, with a whole life before you, is meaningless.

*1 Timothy 3:12*—A deacon must be faithful to his wife, and he must manage his children and household well.

*1 Thessalonians 5:23*—Now may the God of peace make you holy in every way, and may your whole spirit and soul and body be kept blameless until our Lord Jesus Christ comes again.

*2 Thessalonians 3:8*—We never accepted food from anyone without paying for it. We worked hard day and night so we would not be a burden to any of you.

Also take a moment to look up Daniel 1, 6:10-11 as the passages are too long to quote in their entirety. Daniel is a wonderful example of a young man following God devotedly who took care of his physical body as a part of his spiritual health. Daniel and his friends show the king a better way to live through eating only vegetables. His prayer life was disciplined and his overall story presents a picture of discipline in all areas of life.

Do you find that you have balance in your life? Stop now to review your schedule for the past week. Did you have times of rest, family time, healthy eating, exercise, prayer, and household management? There are many reasons people do not care for themselves. We will address these in Chapter 6 when we discuss specific traps that you may find in this area of emotional health.

I once saw a clip of the Bob Newhart show in which he was a therapist. A woman came into his office and she explained to him her phobia of enclosed spaces. Bob looked at her and said, "I know what you need to do. STOP IT!" She said, "But, I'm not sure..." and again Bob yelled, "JUST STOP IT!" She ultimately left his office, as anyone would if this was their experience in a counselor's office.

Too often, Christians take this approach and even at times use Scripture to make the point. As we take a deeper look at these areas of emotional health, please do not be tempted to beat yourself up or read the Bible in such a way that you feel consumed by guilt. Your entire life and spiritual journey centers on Jesus, not on you. So don't be so hard on yourself! Growth takes time, and as you take note of problem areas in your life, avoid lecturing yourself or giving up because you don't feel good enough. You are not good enough! None of us are. This need for a Savior is what joins us all together on the journey.

In this book we are not just asking, "What do I need to do to be emotionally healthy?" You may know *what* the Bible says you ought to do but you have no idea *how* to go about changing. Change is very hard, especially when there is emotional brokenness involved. At the end of each chapter you will find a section called *Next Steps*. This will highlight specific ideas for moving forward on the various issues described and will make connections to the Bible for those struggling with an emotional trap. We will focus on the *how* of change in addition to identifying *what* to change. Additionally, Chapter 7 will provide some suggestions on moving forward.

# 2

## THINKING:
## UNDERSTANDING INSIGHT AND
## SELF-AWARENESS

Early in our marriage my husband and I needed a second car. We were not looking for something that would last; it was really just needed for a semester internship. After finding an ad for a used car for sale by owner, we went cash-in-hand and bought the car for a few hundred dollars. The car appeared to run decently, especially for such an old car, but it did have one problem: the engine temperature gauge was broken. No matter how long we left that car on, the needle would hang lifelessly below the "C." Considering that we did not really need the car for very long, we did not bother having the gauge fixed. About six weeks into owning that car, however, I was driving when the car began to overheat. With a broken gauge, I continued to drive the car unsuspectingly until it began to struggle, finally dying at a stoplight, never to run again. The engine had been completely destroyed because I had driven it overheated. All because of that little tiny, lifeless needle.

Oftentimes, a person's thinking is like that car gauge. Life seems to be running fine, but when problems arise there is no warning that something is off. This person has a lack of insight and self-awareness. They do not see themselves with emotional balance; they are either all right or all wrong. Many times, a person struggling in this area of emotional health has problems with self-esteem – feeling insecure, worthless, and worrying what others are thinking of them. On the other extreme, there are also those who have a more grandiose picture of themselves – they are unable to see when they are wrong, often overwhelm others socially, and are unable to take into consideration the views of others. On both ends of the spectrum, the person who has unhealth in the area of thinking can often be self-absorbed and struggle socially.

Let's take a more detailed look at some of the specific traps related to unhealthy thinking. I will be referencing the Diagnostic and Statistical Manual of Mental Disorders, Fifth Edition (2013) frequently to provide information related to more severe disorders. This manual is commonly known as the DSM-5 and provides diagnostic categories in which certain types of emotional symptoms are grouped together. I find the DSM-5 to be a helpful tool in order to understand various ways in which certain symptoms (like anxiety) present in different ways for different people. Most of you reading this book will not experience symptoms at this level, and the goal is certainly not to label yourself or give yourself a "pass" on spiritual growth because you meet the criteria for a specific disorder. If anything, I find the opposite to be true in my counseling practice: when I understand the type and severity of emotional or psychological issue I am addressing, I can help move the person more effectively towards change and growth. So let's take a look at some specific types of unhealthy thinking.

## NEGATIVE THINKING

"I'm just no good." "I'll never amount to much." "I feel so hopeless and worthless." "Life will never get any better." "I don't really enjoy life anymore." "I just want to die." These are the types of statements you will hear from someone with negative thinking patterns. Sometimes these negative thoughts are for a brief period of time; the person is normally upbeat but is going through what counselors might call a "depressive episode." Some people have recurring depressive episodes throughout their lifetime. For some, negative thoughts define a person's entire way of thinking and those around them would agree that they have a long-standing negative view of the world. Our childhood friend, Eeyore, is an example of this level of negative thinking.

Not all negative thinking is the same. As you reflect on your own negative thinking patterns, think through these levels of severity: venting, currently depressed, chronically depressed, chronically negative. Have you ever been in a venting state? (I know I have!) In this case, you will most likely feel better and change your way of thinking after talking through the issue. For the most part, you are stable in your thinking, and you may even find yourself surprised to hear yourself talking so negatively.

On the other hand, someone in the midst of a depressed episode (what I am calling "currently depressed") will have at least two weeks of symptoms such as feelings of worthlessness and hopelessness, lack of interest in activities they once enjoyed, sleeping problems, weight loss or gain, low mood, and possibly suicidal thinking.[1] If your symptoms seem to fall into this category, it is critical to seek medical and psychological evaluation as medication and professional counseling will likely help you tremendously.

Someone who is "chronically depressed" experiences the above symptoms repeatedly throughout their life and has most likely already received some type of medication and mental health treatment. If this is you, it is important to have a life-long maintenance plan: continue medication and counseling indefinitely.

Finally, a person who is "chronically negative" would be the "Eeyore" of the crowd: nothing is ever good enough, he or she is consistently disappointed by life and feels there is nothing he or she can do to change life circumstances. The person who is chronically negative will find change very difficult, but with the right counselor and strategic therapeutic interventions, this person can begin to move towards the biblical model of healthy thinking as described in Chapter 1.

How does negative thinking relate to the discipleship process? Let's consider Janet, with

---

[1] American Psychiatric Association. (2013). *Diagnostic and Statistical Manual of Psychiatric Disorders* (5th ed.). Arlington, VA: American Psychiatric Publishing.

whom I have worked for several years. She falls into the "chronically depressed" category and came to me after a psychiatric hospitalization resulting from a suicide attempt. Janet is a Christian who has been on-and-off depressed for about 30 years. She has received every type of mental health service possible and often these have saved her life. Despite these services and ongoing medication, her symptoms were not improving. When she came to me, I understood why she continued to struggle—her main source of unresolved negative thinking stemmed from a fear that she was "not really saved." When she looked around her at church, she saw seemingly happy people who could handle life and had joy in their hearts. "Aren't Christians supposed to have love and joy in their hearts? I don't have that so I must not really be a Christian."

Janet had not been able to get help in answering this question. Her pastor had tried lovingly reassuring her that she was indeed a Christian, but was not able to respond to the problem she faced because he could not fully understand her mental illness. Why wasn't she feeling love and joy? Does that mean there is something spiritually wrong with her? Those are the fruit of the Spirit, right? Likewise, Janet's secular counselors had been unable to help with this particular area. They had done a great job of crisis planning and symptom management, but as unbelievers they were unable to address this complicated question.

For Janet, an understanding of the connection between mental health and the discipleship process was critical. Over the course of a year or two, I was able to help Janet stop using words like, "should" and "ought," stop comparing her own spiritual life to others, and to come to terms with what we called her "feelings disorder." Janet could not move forward spiritually unless she stopped using comparison to others as her grid for assessing her own spiritual state. Moving her eyes from her own feelings of inadequacy onto the adequacy of Christ's mercy was key. Because of the broken world in which we live, she suffers from a chronic physical problem in her brain that disrupts the normal flow of feelings. Janet must rest her spiritual understandings on knowledge and faith rather than on how much she feels love or joy.

The fruit of the Spirit is not a list of feelings. When depressed feelings or negative thinking get in the way, you can still act in faith and obedience and be filled with the Spirit of God. The peace and hope of Christ gives you the freedom to seek healing and believe that there is more for you beyond your feelings and circumstances. When your focus shifts from yourself onto the truth of Christ and onto serving others, He can pull you from that dark place.

## ANXIOUS THINKING

While some like Janet struggle with negative and depressed thinking, others face daily anxiety that some may label "worry." There are various types of anxious thinking, including common anxiety, generalized anxiety, panic specific anxiety including social anxiety, and anxiety related to trauma. We will address trauma-linked anxiety in Chapter 5 related to a person's past. Here we will focus on the first four listed.

Common anxiety is the term I am using to mean anxiety that is not life-controlling but is present either in times of stress or even in calm periods. This low-level type of anxiety is experienced by most of us at some point in our lives, generally before, during, or after a major life change. We may feel worried about making the right decision, or be anxious that our children will not mature as we hoped. Common anxiety is... well, common. It is likely you will experience this at points in your life.

You may be thinking, "Well, the Bible says not to be anxious about anything, so I just need trust God more. I must not be a very good

Christian." While we can absolutely grow in our ability to give these worries to God, the method of telling an anxious person (including yourself) to cast their cares on God (with no other strategic interventions) falls short and is the equivalent to the Bob Newhart "Stop it!" method described earlier. Don't do this to yourself, and do not say this to a friend struggling with anxiety. If you have experienced anxiety, you probably have wanted to stop feeling anxious but you may not have known how. Watch out for simplistic answers; seek professional Christian counseling to develop strategies for coping and changing your thinking patterns as the means of surrendering all of yourself to God.

Generalized anxiety is the form of anxiety most often called "worrying" and this is seen when a person has anxiety related to a broad range of daily activities. This person may be seen as pessimistic, always sure that something bad will happen to him/herself or family members/friends. In order to be diagnosed clinically, the anxiety must feel out of the person's control. A person with generalized anxious thinking also will likely struggle with sleeping problems, tiredness, muscle tension, difficulty concentrating, and irritability.[2] Panic

---

[2] Ibid.

attacks can be connected to generalized anxiety but are often found in isolation. With panic, the majority of the time a person's thinking is not particularly anxious, but he or she experiences a sudden onset of physical symptoms such as shortness of breath, sweaty palms, dizziness, heart palpitations, and fears of dying as a result of the episode.

Some with anxiety experience more specific types of anxiety, including fear of social embarrassment (Social Anxiety Disorder) or a specific phobia such as fear of flying, snakes, blood, etc. Usually this kind of anxious thinking prevents a person from engaging in certain activities. I have met many people who have a very difficult time going to church because of social anxiety; they really hate shaking everyone's hand and engaging in small talk! The impact of social anxiety on a person's spiritual life can be devastating as they are unable to build support networks, join Bible studies, or develop relationships with other Christians.

One of the most important things to note about common and specific anxious thinking is that much of the time the person is aware that his or her thinking is irrational but is not able to stop. In the case of generalized anxiety, the person may feel that their worries are rational and likely to happen, even when others around them would perceive reality differently. Anxiety is a real, physical disorder that the person usually wants to eliminate but is unsure how to go about changing.

In my opinion the worst approach for anxiety is to try to reason with yourself. You will not be able to talk yourself out of anxiety. Medication can also be a dangerous route as many anti-anxiety medications are addictive (although some anti-depressants could be helpful for certain types of anxiety symptoms and these are typically not addictive). For severe, life-controlling anxiety, medication may be necessary. For those with a more manageable form of anxious thinking, physical coping skills are critical. Activities such as deep-breathing exercises, meditation on the Bible, relaxation, and positive thinking are some of the types of interventions that can be beneficial.

## OBSESSIVE THINKING

In the DSM-5 classification, there are two distinct types of obsessive thinking: Obsessive Compulsive Disorder and Obsessive Compulsive Personality Disorder. For those not diagnosable with one of these disorders, there are some who find themselves struggling with an inability to "move on" or "get over" various events or circumstances. We will call this type of thinking "ruminating" and I want to distinguish this from those who are healing from a trauma or guilt from their past, as this will be addressed in Chapter 5.

Ruminating can be a major hindrance to spiritual growth, as the person struggling with even this low-level of obsessive thinking can be easily stuck and unable to move on in their thinking. This person may hold a grudge, be unable to make decisions, or have a need for control. Spiritually, the person dealing with ruminating may have difficulty getting along with others in ministry. They might be likely to be very responsible, conscientious, and rule-following but in ministries where flexibility and team-playing are needed this person will create conflict.

Those with more life-controlling Obsessive Compulsive Disorder (OCD) find their entire life consumed with repeating thoughts and routines. Usually, a person with OCD recognizes that these thoughts and rituals are irrational, but finds himself totally unable to stop.[3] You can imagine the difficulty of spiritual growth when nearly every moment of one's day is impacted by repetitive thinking and behavior.

Similarly named but very different in

---

[3] Ibid.

symptomatic presentation is Obsessive Compulsive Personality Disorder. This disorder is not characterized by repetitive routines and obsessive thoughts, but is more like the description of ruminating to an extreme level. This person will present as very rigid, placing rules, details, morals, and perfection above all else in an extreme fashion. Sometimes a person with Obsessive Compulsive Personality Disorder seeks to control others and can become abusive or even obsessed with controlling another person to the point of stalking.

If you have any type of obsessive thinking, you might struggle in your spiritual life due to frustrations with your church context. You might find yourself unable to let go of specific issues in the church, such as the volume or style of music or a ministry leader that rubs you the wrong way. Being aware of the way your obsessive thinking impacts your church experience can help you move through these issues and fight the impulse to leave in frustration.

**GRANDIOSE THINKING**

The word "grandiose" is defined as "affectedly grand or important... more complicated or elaborate than necessary."[4] While

---

[4] Retrieved March 9, 2014 from www.dictionary.com.

there are three diagnosable disorders in this category, there are likely many who may not fit a diagnosis but display features of grandiose thinking. In this case, you may have *inflated* thinking. Some might label this "pride" or "arrogance" as you speak more highly of yourself than perhaps is warranted. If you think more highly of yourself than your friends think of you, you may have inflated thinking. Here there is an apparent disconnect between your view of your own abilities and what you are truly capable of. You may be unable to see your own weaknesses even if they are gently pointed out.

More severe forms of grandiose thinking can be seen in specific symptoms that occur in defined episodes. Someone meeting the criteria for a *hypomanic* episode according to the DSM-5 would display at least three of the following symptoms for 4 days or more: inflated self-esteem, decreased need for sleep, more talkative than usual, racing or loosely connected thoughts, distractibility, increase in goal-directed activity, and increased engagement in pleasurable activities that could have negative consequences, such as sex or spending. For a *manic* episode, you would experience these same symptoms but they would occur for at least a week and with greater severity and greater threat of danger.[5]

One of the most pervasive and severe disorders involving grandiose thinking is Histrionic Personality Disorder. As with all personality disorders, change and insight are extremely difficult and you may not be fully helped with mood stabilizing medication. A person meeting the DSM-5 criteria for Histrionic Personality Disorder would display the following symptoms: must be center of attention, sexually inappropriate or provocative, shallow and rapidly shifting emotions, draws attention to self with physical appearance, speech is grand but lacking depth of meaning, dramatic or theatrical in presentation, easily influenced by others, and perceiving relationships to be more intimate than they are.[6] Someone meeting the full criteria would demonstrate five or more of these symptoms over a several-year period of time. Unlike hypomania and mania, Histrionic Personality Disorder does not occur in episodes but is a pervasive and consistent pattern of behavior.

Spiritually, grandiose thinking will prevent growth because you do not have an

[5] American Psychiatric Association. (2013). *Diagnostic and Statistical Manual of Psychiatric Disorders* (5th ed.). Arlington, VA: American Psychiatric Publishing.
[6] Ibid.

accurate understanding of yourself. Sometimes grandiose talk actually reflects a fragile self-image, subconsciously propped up by exaggerated language. You may have come to believe that you are better than most people you meet or more capable than others around you. While grandiose thinking may seem like pride, inwardly it is an inability to face who you fear you may be.

## A WORD ABOUT DIAGNOSABLE DISORDERS

You should not try to diagnose yourself with any type of disorder. I have provided this information to describe the spectrum on which disrupted thinking can occur. If you think you have some of these symptoms, see a professional Christian counselor or a doctor who can properly evaluate you. If you notice symptoms, it is important to consider the degree to which the symptoms bother you. Also, you should consider the frequency, intensity, and duration of the symptoms. If any of these "thinking" symptoms we've discussed are occurring very frequently (more days than not), are intense (7 or higher on a scale of 1-10), and last for lengthy periods of time (2 weeks or more) you are likely going to need to see a professional.

## A NOTE ABOUT SUICIDAL THINKING

If you have wishes for death or desires or plans to harm yourself, seek immediate help at an emergency room, or call 9-1-1 or the National Suicide Prevention Lifeline  at 1-800-273-8255. Such feelings are not normal and require professional evaluation.

## NEXT STEPS

Now that we have taken an in-depth look at various types of thinking problems, you are probably wondering what to do next. Here are some ideas to get you started:

**Define your spiritual life in terms of *knowledge* and *actions* as opposed to feelings.** When thinking is off, feelings about yourself and others can be off. As with Janet, who I described earlier in this chapter, people who do not *feel* love or joy in normal ways often believe they are spiritually inferior. This sets them up to constantly compare themselves to others and keeps the focus on the self.  On the other hand, a grandiose thinker may feel he is very spiritually mature but has little knowledge of the Bible and is not in obedience to the Word. For any of us, feeling close to God is not a good indicator of our spiritual standing. Trust in the word of God and demonstration of obedience are more accurate measures.

> *Proverbs 3:5-6*—Trust in the LORD with all your heart and lean not on your own understanding; in all your ways submit to him, and he will make your paths straight (NIV).

**Acknowledge the physical issues.** If you are an anxious or obsessive thinker you may really want to trust God more fully, but you are stuck spiritually because you feel you cannot. Having a physical anxiety disorder does not mean you cannot trust God or grow spiritually. It simply means that your body is not sending the right signals. Identify ways in which you do demonstrate trust in God in your daily life, perhaps by taking steps of faith that are challenging or obeying God's word. Again, physical feelings are not a good representation of spiritual standing. If you feel anxious but wish you did not feel this way, your mind and body are not working together correctly. As in the verse below, we can focus on the heart issues rather than the physical symptoms. Can you in your more rational moments declare your true belief and trust in God? Do you seek the heart of God?

*Psalm 139:23-24*—Search me, God, and know my heart; test me and know my anxious thoughts. See if there is any offensive way in me, and lead me in the way everlasting (NIV).

**Ask for feedback.** Seek a pastor, mentor, or counselor's feedback on your behavior and thinking patterns. Open yourself to what they may have to say rather than becoming defensive or arguing with them. Getting an outside perspective will help you uncover blind spots and help you increase your insight.

*Hebrews 12:11*—No discipline is enjoyable while it is happening—it's painful! But afterward there will be a peaceful harvest of right living for those who are trained in this way.

**Improve self-awareness.** I would encourage almost anyone to practice self-awareness strategies to improve thinking patterns. If you do not know what you are thinking and feeling, you will not know why you act the way you do. There are two great ways to practice self-awareness: journaling and self-observation. Write down your observations about your interactions with others, or the thoughts you have about yourself.

Separate these thoughts into "truth" versus "lies." Satan wants to keep you trapped in poor thought patterns to prevent you from experiencing true freedom in Christ. Read on to Chapter 7 for more specific tips on how to practice journaling and self-observation.

> *Proverbs 2:3*—Cry out for insight, and ask for understanding.

# 3

# RELATIONSHIPS: PATTERNS, NETWORKS, AND INFLUENCES

Just in the last week, I have sat with three different women in my counseling office who allowed an abuser from their past to move back into their homes. "But he's my son, I can't turn him out to the streets..." says one. "I'm trying not to get my hopes up this time..." says another. The third told me, "He didn't really ask, he just told me he was moving his stuff in." I told them all I was angry for them. Yet I heard and understood their pain; saying "no" is easier said than done. A glimmer of hope that someone you love might change is a powerful force that often overrides our better judgment. And as all three of these women could attest, getting out of an unhealthy relationship is even harder than staying out of one in the first place.

Relationship problems are a common issue found in churches, with unfortunately too few truly healthy families in our midst. More often than not, even the relationships that appear healthy on Sunday morning are quite different the rest of the week. Tragically some of these are pastors' families, paralyzed by the drive to present a perfect model to the church yet driven apart by ministry demands. When a person's relationships are unhealthy, spiritual growth is difficult at best. If we cannot love our brother, how can we love God? We continuously sin against ourselves and against each other in unhealthy relationships, causing an ongoing divide between ourselves and God. And our relationship with God will resemble our relationships with others and take on its own unhealthy patterns.

In this chapter we will look at four specific relationship traps, and we will also examine social networks and influences. To understand relationship dynamics, we will look at the degree of closeness in relationships as well as the degree of conflict. The end of each of these continuums will provide helpful categories by which to understand relationship traps. Other writers, such as Dr. David Olson, have presented more complex models specific to couple relationships which you may find helpful for more specific relationship systems.[7] At the end of this chapter you will also find a *Next Steps* section for specific suggestions on how to address relationship traps as you seek to grow spiritually.

## IMBALANCED RELATIONSHIPS

Codependency, enmeshment, closeness, lack of boundaries. These terms are commonly used about relationships, but sometimes the definition of each is lost in its overuse or misuse. To simplify and define for our purposes, I am using *imbalanced relationships* to describe those in which there is not a mutual give-and-take in the relationship and where relationship roles are confused or inappropriate. On the closeness spectrum, imbalanced relationships tend to be too close and as a result there are not clear roles. People in these relationships give or take too much from each other and this typically results in anxiety, frustration, cycles of conflict, and ultimately crisis in the relationship.

---

[7] Olson, D. H., Sprenkle, D. H. and Russell, C. S. (1979). "Circumplex Model of Marital and Family Systems: I. Cohesion and Adaptability Dimensions, Family Types, and Clinical Applications." *Family Process*, 18: 3–28.

Friends, parent/child, and couple relationships can all fall into the category of *imbalanced*. The underlying issues with imbalanced relationships often stem from a belief that one person can change the other. Boundaries are set aside in order to "help" the person change, yet this backfires when the same patterns continue. As we look at some examples in this category, keep in mind some of the thinking traps we discussed in the last chapter. With all the emotional traps we discuss, you will find overlap as one area of unhealth leads to another.

Let's take a look at Betsy. She is an 11-year-old girl whose parents are divorced, and she often finds herself being used as a go-between. Her father sends messages to her mother through Betsy, and Betsy's mother often shares deep personal feelings and secrets with her. Betsy is experiencing enmeshed relationships. She has been put in an adult role, creating imbalance as the child is elevated and the adults are putting the emotional weight of their problems onto her. This imbalance puts Betsy in a position in which she most likely cannot be honest with her parents, begins to view herself as more capable than her parents, and is not having her own emotional needs met. Her parents are placing their own needs above hers.

` Similarly, an adult child who has inappropriate expectations of his parents can create an imbalanced relationship as well. This can happen frequently when parents feels they have made mistakes and have negatively impacted the grown child's life. Their own guilt can cause them to give the adult child what he wants, such as money or housing. Perhaps the pattern of an inability to say "no" has been there throughout the child's life, thus creating the system in which he continues to demand more and avoid personal responsibility.

Couples can have imbalanced relationships as well. One partner might dominate the other, making demands and unable to give respect to the other partner. The imbalanced couple may have a pattern of breaking up and resuming the relationship repeatedly. This pattern will lead to instability as the give-and-take imbalance is not sustainable. In addition, you may see one member of the couple bringing in a third party to the relationship, such as a mother, child, or friend. Addictions, the focus of the next chapter, can be at the root of imbalanced relationships as well.

Perhaps you are single, but your relationships with friends seem imbalanced. You may make friends very quickly, meeting a person and within a week or two being "best friends." Just as quickly, you stop speaking to the person due to conflict or feeling that you have been taken advantage of. There is a pattern of these unstable relationships, and typically the people in your life are not helping you move forward spiritually. Unfortunately, churches can sometimes foster imbalanced friend relationships by encouraging rapid trust. In these cases, one person "serving" another can become unsustainable or unhealthy.

When assessing this area, it is important to ask: What is each person getting out of the relationship? Can each person express honestly how they feel? Is one person actively seeking to get his own needs met above the other person's? What boundaries are in place that prevent imbalance? It is important to take note of when you tend to say "yes" when other people might set a boundary, or on the other extreme when you tend to take more than you give in your relationships.

## ISOLATION

On the opposite end of the closeness spectrum is isolation. Here we find those some might label "loners" or those who seem to feel they do not need others. Be careful not to stereotype isolation; you may be the classic quiet, withdrawn person or you may feel that if you want things done right you can only trust yourself to get the job done. Finding the root cause of isolation is the key; what is the underlying anxiety preventing you from engaging in trusting relationships?

In the most mild case of isolation, a person may simply tend towards introversion. Others may see you as aloof or distant, when in reality you simply feel more comfortable alone or feel drained by being around other people. At times an introverted person may seem shy until they feel comfortable in a social setting. You may feel a bit socially awkward, with a dislike of "small talk" and with an aversion to "loud" personalities. For the shy or introverted, plugging in to a small group or ministry may help you develop relationships in your church.

For some, introversion is not the cause of isolation, but rather there may be problems from a lack of trust in others. This mistrust could be caused by trauma, including verbal or emotional abuse. Additionally, the inability to trust could stem from a past relationship that caused significant hurt.

Those who have experienced this level of pain in relationships need significant emotional and spiritual healing. This will require more than just a few sessions of counseling as you work to build a new trusting relationship. I once had a client for whom it took almost 2 years before she was able to trust me fully! Because of severe emotional abuse as a child, she was very resistant to trusting an authority or parental type figure in her life. It takes time for someone who has been abused or emotionally wounded to begin to trust again.

Sadly, sometimes we do not reach the point of true healing because either the client or the counselor gives up too quickly. When you do not want to trust you may subconsciously find ways to try to sabotage the relationship, including blaming others or being angry with someone trying to help you. These feelings, often known as "transference" in healing relationships, have much more to do with past relationships than they do with your new, present relationships. Be careful to not give up too quickly on new relationships or find reasons to stop trusting.

For more severe forms of isolation in relationships, we turn again to the DSM-5 to take a look at diagnosable levels of social isolation. Social Anxiety Disorder is characterized by a fear of embarrassment in public, anxiety when anticipating a feared social situation, and avoidance of anxiety provoking social situations.

A person with this diagnosis will recognize that the fears are irrational and will observe disruption in daily life because of the symptoms.[8]

No matter what the underlying cause, when you are noticing isolation you want to assess the intensity and duration. Is the isolation so intense that you feel incapable of making any friends? Are you willing to begin a trusting relationship in a controlled setting such as a counselor's office? How long has it been since you have had meaningful relationships? Even if you prefer to remain isolated or are happier by yourself, it is important to recognize that humans were designed for relationships. The first thing God noticed after making one person was that it was not good for him to be alone. Those who remain in isolation are at higher risk for depression and impaired thinking patterns.

## HIGH-CONFLICT RELATIONSHIPS

There are many types of high-conflict relationships. All have a common thread: loud and harmful levels of conflict that breed mistrust and pain. Frequent yelling, destruction of property, and even police involvement are

---

[8] American Psychiatric Association. (2013). *Diagnostic and Statistical Manual of Psychiatric Disorders* (5th ed.). Arlington, VA: American Psychiatric Publishing.

characteristic of high-conflict relationships. The four levels of high-conflict relationships are the following: *angry, chaotic, addiction-related*, and *abusive*.

Some high-conflict relationships are *angry*. In this level of conflict, there is no physical violence or destruction of property, but there is plenty of yelling and name-calling. Stress and past wounds are often at the root of angry relationships. If you are constantly worried, stressed, or feeling at the end of your rope, you are far more likely to yell or snap at the next person who walks across your path. If you are on the receiving end, you may have asked someone a question or made a seemingly innocuous remark only to be yelled at or verbally attacked.

For other high-conflict relationships, the root cause may be an overall pattern of chaos. In *chaotic* relationships conflict arises when patterns repeat over and over, particularly when these patterns could seemingly have been avoided. For example, a couple I once knew in counseling were constantly arguing over money and the husband's job status. It seemed that the husband could not keep a steady job but spent money very freely. The chaos from the constant lack of reliability and ongoing financial strain would never be solved in any one argument. The systemic problems in chaotic relationships often need both individual counseling for each person in the relationship as well as marriage or family counseling to address relationship patterns.

Beyond general life chaos, some high-conflict relationships are characterized by addiction issues. These *addiction-related* relationships involve one or more people addicted to drugs, alcohol, sex, money/gambling, food, or technology. Conflict usually centers around the impact of addictive behavior on others and on the quality of the relationship. Frequently addiction-related relationships involve some level of codependency or enabling as the non-addicted member continually seeks to rescue the addict.

Finally, *abusive* high-conflict relationships are ones in which physical violence, property destruction, loud name-calling, belittling, or public shaming are part of the conflict cycle. One or both parties in the relationship may be engaging in these abusive behaviors. Some have a clear abuser and victim, while others have patterns of abuse from both sides. This type of relationship may be the *angry* type initially, but as conflict increases the relationship may become abusive as each fight "ups the ante" and more severe actions become a part of the conflict.

## AVOIDANT RELATIONSHIPS

In contrast to high-conflict relationships, avoidant relationships tend to minimize, avoid, or hide conflict. Do not be mistaken—conflict is present in avoidant relationships. But instead of yelling or escalated arguing, avoidant relationships involve acting as if everything is fine when clearly there are problems. Avoidant relationships can be abusive as well, but are more likely to involve secretive abuse such as emotional abuse (manipulation) or sexual abuse. There are four types of avoidant relationships: *inexpressive, pretending, fragile,* and *abusive.*

*Inexpressive* avoidant relationships are characterized by an inability to express feelings or opinions. One or both parties involved in the relationship may simply not know how to express desires or feelings. This leads to a lack of outward conflict despite the deep inward conflict or discontentment felt. The lack of ability to express oneself may stem from a basic lack of assertiveness skills, or there may be past hurt from previous attempts to express feelings that were shut down by another person. As a result, the person unable to express him or herself may feel a great deal of conflict about the relationship, but the other person may have no idea that there are any problems. When these problems are allowed to silently fester, there may come an explosion point that comes as a great surprise to the other person who believed everything was fine.

In *pretending* avoidant relationships, there is more awareness of problems or conflict, but the conflict is actively hidden from outsiders. If you have been in a relationship or family system like this, you may have felt a great disconnect between private and public behavior. In contrast to high-conflict relationships, who may be overheard by neighbors or passers by, pretending relationships have a high fear of judgment by others. As a result, great care is taken to keep up appearances and ensure that any conflict is safely hidden.

This type of relationship breeds dishonesty, lying, and hypocrisy, as the true reality of the relationship is never allowed to be revealed. This can also be a barrier in seeking help for relationship problems. I have had clients come into my office for couple's or family counseling and tell me everything is fine. If that were the case, they would not be in my office!

A third type of avoidant relationship, the *fragile* type, involves active efforts to make everything "okay" in the relationship to prevent or smooth over conflict. In these relationships, problems are not actually solved, but rather covered up with a Band-aid approach. Typically there is one member of the relationship who has a deep-seated fear of abandonment. Any time conflict arises, this person ends up taking the fall, apologizing regardless of fault, and taking action to make sure there are no hard feelings. This behavior perpetuates the cycle of conflict because the one who fears abandonment continually prevents the other person from owning their mistakes or apologizing. Over time the relationship becomes lopsided and can develop into an aggressor/victim pattern.

As with high-conflict relationships, avoidant relationships can be *abusive* as well. This abuse is more likely to be of a manipulative or secretive nature, such as emotional abuse or sexual abuse. In abusive avoidant relationships, the abuser may threaten the victim if he or she reveals the abuse. The abuser is likely to be in denial about his or her actions and the harm that they are causing. Police involvement is less common than in high-conflict relationships because victims may not come forward out of fear or shame. Abusers in avoidant relationships take great care to ensure that no one finds out about the abuse.

### NETWORKS AND INFLUENCES

In addition to evaluating the types of relationships you are in, it is important to assess your networks and influences. Your networks are your social circles as well as your family and other supports. Your relational influences are any relationships that help move you forward or ones that pull you backwards. In my book titled *Getting Your Life Under Control,* I described in detail the concept of family systems and social systems. Here I will more briefly explore options for finding positive supports and influences, and I will describe negative supports and influences.

Take a moment to think about who you would write down on a list of supports. To whom do you go when you are upset or need advice? Are you engaged in a church or any social clubs? Do your networks drive you to grow, or are they plagued by some of the unhealthy relationship patterns we have talked about throughout this chapter? Are your influences bringing you to greater heights or keeping you stuck in old patterns?

Positive networks and influences are ones in which you feel you can grow and develop. Examples would be relationships like an encouraging mentor or pastor, a friend who respects your boundaries and demonstrates that he or she is trustworthy. Positive family systems have clear communication, healthy boundaries, and respect among all members.

Negative networks and influences are

often tied to your past. If you have become a Christian or returned to God in adulthood, some of your old networks are likely to influence you away from God. When you remain tied to these networks, your growth is stunted and you eventually find you cannot move forward emotionally or spiritually. There may also be specific sins that you engaged in with these networks. You will likely be drawn back into sin as negative influences take hold of you.

You need more than one network. At least two circles, such as family, friends or church will provide balance in your life. Just as the American government runs on three distinct branches to provide a checks-and-balances system, so too your life needs multiple networks to provide a balance of perspectives. Within your networks, it is also helpful to have people from other cultures or ethnic groups so that you can avoid becoming stuck in one limited way of thinking.

## NEXT STEPS

Making changes to your relationships can be difficult and painful. Here are some suggestions that can serve as a roadmap for change. Don't try to make all of these changes now, but one step at a time. Focus on slow and steady growth.

**Practice relationship skills.** This includes communication skills like assertiveness and listening as well as boundary setting and conflict resolution skills.

> *Matthew 7:12*—Do to others whatever you would like them to do to you. This is the essence of all that is taught in the law and the prophets.

**Identify two positive support sources.** If you can't, write out step-by-step ways to build these by starting with one person you would like to get to know better.

> *Proverbs 17:17*—A friend is always loyal, and a brother is born to help in time of need.

**Develop a trusting relationship with a pastor, mentor, or counselor.** Let this be a model on which you can build another relationship if you struggle with trust.

> *Proverbs 27:9*—The heartfelt counsel of a friend is as sweet as perfume and incense.

**Develop clear boundaries.** This means trusting

those who have shown they will not hurt you and not trusting those you have just met or who have harmed you. Get to know yourself and your own limits. The more deeply you understand your own emotional issues, the more you can begin to identify which problems are yours to solve and which problems belong to someone else.

> *Matthew 5:37*—Just say a simple, 'Yes, I will,' or 'No, I won't.' Anything beyond this is from the evil one.

**Pinpoint influences.** Create a plan to cut out negative influences and use a journal to write about reasons you have had trouble getting rid of these negative influences in the past.

> *Psalm 1:1-2*—Oh, the joys of those who do not follow the advice of the wicked, or stand around with sinners, or join in with mockers. But they delight in the law of the LORD, meditating on it day and night.

# 4

## ADDICTIONS: DEPENDENCY ON SUBSTANCES AND BEYOND

If you have never faced an addiction to illegal drugs or alcohol, you may be tempted to skip ahead to the next chapter. Sadly, addictions are not limited to substances and many struggle with addictions that they have not properly identified. Food, sex, money, and technology have pervaded many modern cultures and hold captive many (even Christians!) who are often unaware of just how enslaved they have become.

The definition of "addiction" is in itself a debate, with some suggesting that addiction is a disease while others have viewed it as a moral failing or sin. In the past 5 to 10 years,, scientific studies have helped us understand the way that a person's brain functions when addicted. While we don't have complete answers as to how addiction works, we do know that many overcome addiction every day. Your brain is certainly involved in and harmed by an addiction, but this does not mean there is no hope for emotional and physical healing.

In this chapter, we will look at *chemical* and *sexual* addictions as well as addictions stemming from *internal stimuli* and those drawing on *external stimuli*. For any addiction, I believe that healing is possible, although the road to recovery may not be an easy one.

## CHEMICAL ADDICTIONS

The word "addiction" perhaps most often calls to mind chemical addictions. In this type of addiction, specific substances are abused to attain a high or sense of escape. The National Institute on Drug Abuse offers a chart on their website (www.drugabuse.gov) overviewing commonly abused drugs and their effects.

While somewhat more socially acceptable, nicotine use is highly addiction that can be very hard to stop. Cigarette smokers or tobacco chewers have a high risk of cancers and other diseases. If you are a Christian who continues to struggle with smoking or tobacco use, it is important to ask yourself: do I really want to give this up? The process of becoming more like Christ is one in which we all continually surrender our lives to God. Because smoking can be very difficult to quit, some people overlook it as a serious addiction and a spiritual stronghold. When you come to a place where you are ready to quit, don't do it alone! Check out www.smokefree.gov or www.cancer.org for tips and support on quitting smoking.

Stimulants are another category of chemically addictive substances. These are known as "uppers" and include cocaine, speed, and methamphetamines. Coffee drinkers, you aren't off the hook here! Caffeine is also a stimulant and certainly an addictive substance. Social acceptance does not make an addiction any less real. As we offer our "bodies as living sacrifices," we give God our entire beings and give up all of our dependencies. This does not have to be done in one instant, but you should begin to wrestle with ideas of anything (not just coffee) that you may be dependent on besides God.

Alcohol is another chemical substance that is certainly addictive. For Christians, the use of alcohol can be a hotly debated topic. Some feel that alcohol in moderation is good for you (even Paul encouraged a little wine to help the ailing stomach) while others believe that due to its addictive properties alcohol should be completely avoided.

At my church, we have a policy of complete alcohol abstinence for all leaders. This stance does not come from a fear of our ministry leaders becoming drunk—many of them have demonstrated they are able to drink very occasionally and responsibly. However, alcohol IS life-controlling for many, particularly in our inner-city context, and it is a stumbling block that can cause someone to fall away from their walk with God. Before you treat alcohol casually, be aware that there are very often people around you who have struggled with alcoholism. You may never know it, but your actions could lead someone down a dangerous path simply by the example you set as a Christian. Be sure you have really grappled with this issue before dismissing your own use of alcohol, casual as it may seem. If you find that it is too hard to give up social drinking, you may have more of a life-controlling problem than you have realized.

There are many other chemical addictions, including opioids like heroin or opium as well as marijuana, prescription drugs, hallucinogens, and a new type of drug commonly known as "bath salts." Most of these substances are highly dangerous and if you are struggling with addictions to these substances you will likely need professional help from a detox and rehab center. We will pause to discuss two of these, marijuana and abused prescription drugs, as they are addictions that can remain hidden while the addict carries on a seemingly functional life.

Marijuana has been defended by many as "natural" or proclaimed to be a non-dangerous drug. Opium and tobacco are "natural" plants as well, yet there is no doubt as to their negative effect on the body. With many states legalizing marijuana, you may find yourself as a Christian giving yourself a pass on stopping your marijuana use. If this is you, take a moment to consider where your philosophies about your drug use have come from. What influences are telling you that marijuana is safe or not necessary to quit? Are you willing to surrender everything in your process of becoming emotionally and spiritually healthy?

Prescription drugs can often be an addiction that goes unseen as tolerance is built up gradually and your doctor may continue to prescribe them. Certainly some obtain prescription drugs illegally, but for those who have a legitimate prescription it can be hard to think of quitting. Those with chronic pain issues or ongoing insomnia may genuinely need relief, yet they become addicted and controlled by the very thing that was supposed to help. If you are prescribed an addictive medication, talk with your doctor. Even if you are taking it as prescribed, you may become out of control as your tolerance for the drug builds. Find out if any alternatives may be available, and if not, be sure to have honest accountability in your life so that you have safeguards preventing you from abusing or overusing these medications.

### SEXUAL ADDICTIONS

While sexual addictions are rarely acknowledged from the pulpit, vast numbers of Christians struggle secretly and silently. Perhaps not everyone's favorite topic, sex is flaunted in our culture and most are exposed inadvertently to some form of soft porn simply by passing billboards or flipping channels. These exposures can come at very young ages, creating a sexual appetite long before our bodies were designed to handle one.

Perhaps the most common addiction among Christian men today is pornography. Gone is the age in which you had to walk into a shady magazine store to buy porn—a simple click of a mouse can connect you in the privacy of your own home or office. Adrenaline kicks in and huge percentages of Christian men (and a surprising number of women) find themselves out of control and trapped in a pornography addiction. I have heard figures as high as 97% of Christian men have struggled with some form of sexual addiction. The popular book titled *Every Man's Battle* by Stephen Arterburn et al. certainly seems to indicate that sexual addiction is not an uncommon struggle.

Sexual addiction reaches way beyond pornography. Short-term affairs, such as the use of prostitutes or a lifestyle of one-night-stands are also a struggle for many. Our society certainly celebrates promiscuous men and women in television shows and advertising. Many Christians would acknowledge these acts as sin, yet we allow our minds and hearts to be influenced and frequently give in to temptation. Addiction is a pattern of behavior. If you find yourself struggling with sex outside of marriage, have you explored the reasons why? Has this become a pattern of behavior that has begun to own your life?

The same could be said for long-term affairs. Some may not view themselves as having a sexual addiction, yet they are involved in a relationship outside of marriage. The word "affair" is often used for relationships carried on by married people with someone other than a spouse. Any type of sexual relationship outside of marriage would fit here. You may not view yourself as an addict, and you have probably never set foot in a recovery meeting. Yet you may be facing a life-controlling problem that is preventing you from moving forward emotionally and spiritually. Making drastic changes to your relationships is extremely difficult, yet healing will only be possible when you lay all of your desires on the altar and surrender them to God.

There are also many types of deviant sexual behavior that can be addictive. I do not need to write an exhaustive list here. If any type of fetish, obsession, or sexual behavior is in your life you probably have carried pain and shame for a long time. You know exactly what you are facing and you do not have to face it alone. You can find Christian sex addiction recovery sites online or you can connect with SLAA or other recovery groups in your area. Professional Christian counseling may also be a place of healing when you are ready to face your addiction and take a step forward.

### INTERNAL STIMULI

There are other types of addictions that I am placing in the category of *internal stimuli* because there is something done to the body internally. Overeating, undereating, and self-harm all produce internal physical sensations that can become addictive.

Overeating is hard to define in American culture as most of us overeat nearly every day. It is possible to consume a vast amount of calories without even feeling that full or binging. New regulations have prompted restaurants to begin listing calories next to menu items.

Someone dealing with a true food addiction not only overeats in the way most Americans do—eating processed or prepared foods that are high in calories—but food addicts also obsess about food, fantasize about food, and become irritable if limits are placed on what and when they can eat. Secrecy is another key to any addiction. Do you find yourself making plans to eat or overeat when no one is around? Do you continue to eat after you are aware of feeling full? These may signal a food addiction.

Other eating disorders are also a type of food addiction. It is ironic to think about anorexia as a food addiction, since there is a lack of food intake, yet the underlying thought processes are the same. There is an obsession about what goes into the body and lots of emotional energy is put into thinking about food. A sense of control is central here and often points to the root cause of the disorder. When you feel out of control, what are some unhealthy ways you try to regain control? For the person struggling with anorexia, the answer is rigidly controlled food intake. Bulimia nervosa combines overeating (or binge eating) with the desire for control and has addictive patterns as well.

Aside from food, other physical stimulation can be addictive. "Cutting" is a common term for a type of self-harm that involves making oneself bleed using razors or other sharp objects. Addictive patterns develop as a person feels a sense of relief, brought on by the chemicals released in the brain from the pain of cutting. Others find this sensation when they pick at their skin or pull out hair. Any type of self-harm is dangerous and requires professional help. If you have engaged in cutting or any form of self-harm, tell someone. Seek a professional Christian counselor who can help you overcome these life-controlling patterns and help you move forward in understanding your value and worth as a child of God and beautiful creation.

### EXTERNAL STIMULI

In contrast to the internal stimulation caused by food addiction or cutting, external stimuli addictions are ones in which something outside the body becomes life-controlling. Technology, gaming, gambling/money, and risky behaviors all fall into this category. Of course, all addiction involves internal stimulation. Your brain's response and dependency are at the heart of all addictions. I have chosen to classify the external stimuli as such in order to distinguish between various forms of behavior.

Technology is all around us. Most of us have multiple devices we use every day—a phone, a tablet, a computer, a television, and/or a gaming system. Parents are facing a generation of children who operate these devices from a very young age. Earlier tonight, my 4-year-old daughter asked, "Mom, can I get a phone when I'm seven?" Um, no. Limits are critical for children and adults as any device with a back-lit screen can be harmful to the brain (and the eyes!) and can become addictive.

Christians often engage in the same cultural practices as the world around them. Being *in* the world but not *of* the world is certainly a challenge, and most of us do not pay attention to our own assumptions or behavior patterns. We are just as tied to our phones, social media, or computers as anyone else in our neighborhood. Pause for a moment and reflect on your use of technology. Imagine not having access to your phone for a day, a week, a month. What feelings arise when you imagine that scenario? Can you fast from social media, turn off your television for a month, or get rid of some of your devices altogether? Your responses to these questions could indicate a life-controlling problem.

Video and computer games are also a common addiction. Teens are most often thought of when gaming is mentioned, but some continue to find themselves addicted to gaming well into their 20s and 30s or beyond. Hours are devoted to playing, and even more hours are spent thinking about playing. Again, obsessive thinking and behavior is key to examining the problem. Has anyone in your life ever told you that you play computer games too much? Has your wife ever gotten upset with you for playing too many video games? If you want to move forward in your Christian walk, it is important to honestly evaluate yourself. If you feel defensive about keeping gaming as a hobby, you may have a life-controlling addiction.

Gambling or obsessions with money are other forms of external stimuli that are addictive. Behavioral psychologists have developed a body of research on various types of reinforcement. If a person is rewarded every time, the activity becomes boring. (A slot machine that always wins is lucrative but not addictive.) If a person never receives a reward, they will also not become addicted because there is no hope of winning. But *intermittent reinforcement* is the most likely to create addiction because behavior is continually repeated in the hopes that this time will be the lucky win. Again, adrenaline and other brain responses are at play as you experience feelings of hope and wait for victory. Gambling is addictive because some people sometimes win.

Money is an idol for many, and can become a form of addiction as you live your life in pursuit of more and more money. How often do you think about money? Do you find yourself daydreaming about having more money? To what degree is your life centered around financial gain? Have you ever done something you thought you'd never do in order to get more money? If you said "yes" to any of these questions, you may have an addiction to money.

Finally, there is a wide array of risky behaviors that create an adrenaline rush and fall into the category of *external stimuli*. Behaviors like riding a bike dangerously in the street or "dare-devil" kinds of acts can be addictive. These behaviors can be addictive because they can provide that rush. When your body becomes dependent on this sensation, you may have to engage in increasingly dangerous activities in order to get the same feeling. Much like chemical addictions, you can build up a tolerance to your own adrenaline and require a higher level of experience to obtain the same effect.

## ADDICTIONS, COPING, AND SHAME

Every addiction has an onset—the beginning of the behavior. Most likely, at the moment of onset addiction was not present. Some addictions, particularly those to cigarettes and some illegal drugs, develop very quickly and sometimes even after just one use. Other addictions develop slowly over time.

Regardless of the type of addiction or its development, we need to go back to the beginning. Where did this behavior come from? What was going on in your life to make you turn to drugs, alcohol, sex, food, money, or technology as a form of escape? Coping is the main concept here. Addictions very often stem from a need to cope. Perhaps you were abused, or in a difficult situation. Maybe you were stressed, depressed, or anxious. Or maybe you were simply influenced by the culture around you. Understanding how and why you began your addiction can be a key to finding the way out.

Shame plays a central role in addiction. Think of addiction as a cycle. It begins with some type of stress that creates a need for temporary escape. You engage in harmful behavior but perhaps even immediately begin to feel a sense of shame. What would I do if anyone found out? As the addictive sensation wears off, you may feel physically and emotionally horrible. This return of pain now joined by shame creates a situation in which you feel you need to escape again. You have become trapped in an endless cycle of escaping from bad feelings.

There is hope for you. First of all, the truth of God's love and grace is available. Yes, even for you. Regardless of what you have done. Stepping into this mind-bending forgiveness is the first step towards healing. Read the Bible, seek God, and seek help. Some churches offer recovery groups, and professional Christian counseling can help as well. End the isolation and connect with positive influences who can teach you a whole new way to live. Read the list of *Next Steps* for step-by-step ideas.

**NEXT STEPS**

Addictions go beyond habits. They are life-controlling and you will not be able to stop a true addiction without help. Becoming aware of your thinking patterns and finding the right kind of help is critical. Here are some ideas to get you started:

**Look for excuses.** In what ways have you justified your behavior? How has denial played a role in keeping you stuck? When we rationalize and justify our actions—"It's not really that bad," or, "I'm not hurting anyone else..."—we remain stuck and our behavior does not change. Pay attention to your thinking to see where denial may be creeping in.

> *1 Corinthians 6:12*—You say, "I am allowed to do anything"—but not everything is good for you. And even though "I am allowed to do anything," I must not become a slave to anything.

**Be honest.** Admit the true nature of your addiction to yourself, God, and at least one other safe person. It may be helpful to begin by writing it down. Start with one sentence: "I have been stuck in addiction to _____." Then make a list of specific habits, thoughts, or behaviors in which you have engaged.

> *Ephesians 5:11*—Take no part in the worthless deeds of evil and darkness; instead, expose them.

**Get help.** Look for a professional Christian counselor in your area who has experience with addiction issues. If you don't know where to look, ask your pastor for a list of counselors in your area, or call Focus on the Family or New Life Ministries as they keep national lists of Christian counselors.

> *Proverbs 20:18*—Plans succeed through good counsel; don't go to war without wise advice.

**Attend support groups.** There are many types of groups for a variety of addictions. Celebrate Recovery is a nationally available Christian group for all types of addictions. Alcoholics Anonymous, Narcotics Anonymous, Overeaters Anonymous, and SLAA groups are widely available. If you cannot find a group, ask your pastor if your church would have resources to start one, led by someone with many years of recovery, a trained pastor, or a professional Christian counselor.

> *1 John 1:6-8*—So we are lying if we say we have fellowship with God but go on living in spiritual darkness; we are not practicing the truth. But if we are living in the light, as God is in the light, then we have fellowship with each other, and the blood of Jesus, his Son, cleanses us from all sin. If we claim we have no sin, we are only fooling ourselves and not living in

the truth.

**Get to the root.** In my previous book, *Getting Your Life Under Control,* I help you explore ways to find the root issue behind addiction. I also have an entire chapter devoted to addictions and options for moving forward. If you are facing addiction, you need specific strategies for coping, self-care, and relapse prevention. My book and many others can offer useful insight as you develop these strategies and avoid Band-aid approaches.

> *Colossians 2:6-7*—And now, just as you accepted Christ Jesus as your Lord, you must continue to follow him. Let your roots grow down into him, and let your lives be built on him. Then your faith will grow strong in the truth you were taught, and you will overflow with thankfulness.

**Develop a daily routine.** Focusing on taking care of yourself will help prevent you from getting into the emotional place that makes you want to act out in addiction. Regular exercise is an absolute must for anyone fighting addiction. Read on to the chapter in this book on self-care or refer to my suggestions in *Getting Your Life Under Control.*

*Romans 12:1-2*—And so, dear brothers and sisters, I plead with you to give your bodies to God because of all he has done for you. Let them be a living and holy sacrifice—the kind he will find acceptable. This is truly the way to worship him. Don't copy the behavior and customs of this world, but let God transform you into a new person by changing the way you think. Then you will learn to know God's will for you, which is good and pleasing and perfect.

# 5

## PAST: UNLOCKING THE CHAINS

The past is such an elusive concept: you can never get to it, yet it can infiltrate your life and consume your present. There is nothing you can do to change your past, yet you may feel immobilized by it in the present. The most common word I hear as a counselor from people dealing with issues from their pasts is "stuck." They can't go back, can't live in the present, and certainly don't feel like they can move forward.

If you have shared this feeling of being frozen in time and trapped in your own story, you probably need some healing from your past. Healing from the past is not only possible, but it is the only thing that can help you move forward into the rest of your life. Often we want to resolve the past, perhaps by changing it or by somehow bringing justice (either to one who has harmed you or to yourself in some form of penance for your past mistakes). Some want questions answered and feel they cannot move forward until answers come. Yet resolution or answered questions are rare, and these are an unlikely route towards healing.

I have used the phrase "moving forward" instead of "moving on." The idea of moving on carries with it connotations of forgetting about the past, ignoring what has happened, or dismissing your feelings about your past. Moving on does not necessarily include a healing process. Moving forward, however, involves working through your past. Acceptance, forgiveness of self or others, decreasing shame, and finding your new sense of identity are all part of moving forward.

In this chapter, we will walk through specific traps that ensnare you and keep you emotionally stuck in the past. *Developmental issues, abuse, traumatic events,* and *past mistakes* are the four key areas we will explore. At the end of the chapter, we will talk about ways to move forward from traps of the past.

### DEVELOPMENTAL ISSUES

Infancy and childhood for some were

wonderful times of nurturing and growth. For others these periods of life were the beginning of a path leading to low self-esteem, identity confusion, anger, mistrust, and pain. We will explore specific areas of abuse and trauma later on in the chapter, but even if you were not abused or have not experienced trauma, you may be trapped in the past from problems throughout your development.

Poor parenting is a very common problem that contributes to developmental issues. As a parent, I am well aware that there are many things out of a parent's control. I also know that therapists have a bad reputation for being quick to blame the parents for all problems. I am not suggesting that everything wrong in your life is the fault of your parents. But we must acknowledge the reality that some parents have a greater skill set than others, and it may not always be outwardly obvious who those poor parents are.

Sadly, sometimes we may judge a parent's skills by socioeconomic status rather than character. In wealthy families, parents may have more education or be able to present themselves well in public. In poorer families, there is likely to be a lower education level and from the outside we may primarily notice a lack of new clothes or fancy toys. However, a parent's level of engagement with their children and the model they set forth is far more critical to development than a parent's ability to provide materially.

If your parents were disengaged or emotionally unavailable, or if they simply did not know how to handle your behavior, then you may continue to be impacted by these issues today. You may have difficulty trusting others or you may find yourself getting into unhealthy relationships, repeating the same patterns over and over again. You may never have learned coping skills or basic life management skills such as time or money management. You may find yourself emotionally unavailable to your own children, perhaps unsure how to express love or affection to them or to your spouse.

Other developmental issues come as you develop your social network. Being bullied at school or feeling "different" can lead to emotional problems that are the result of getting stuck on a particular developmental stage. Identity formation is a critical developmental stage, particularly throughout middle school and high school. When you have been teased, ostracized, or detached from your peers, you can develop difficulty trusting others or underlying anger. You may find yourself simply disinterested in forming adult relationships. You may believe that the risk in trusting others is not worth any potential gain.

Other social network complications can come from moving a lot as a child. Military families, children in and out of foster care, and families that frequently move due to jobs or financial problems all have the potential to face lasting emotional damage. Children who have to continually try to make new friends or adjust to new schools are often left out of peer groups or simply avoid attachment for fear of loss. If in adulthood, you subconsciously push away relationships as soon as they reach a certain level of closeness, or you dare unable to tolerate a more intimate relationship, you may have an underlying fear of "getting too close."

Isolation in childhood development can also occur when physical handicaps or cultural prejudice are present. Stereotyping or racial profiling can create very deep wounds and anger, as well as internalization of issues that are out of your control. Comparing yourself to others, wishing you were different, or hating yourself can be results of these painful experiences. You may also find that isolation continues into adulthood, as even adults judge you or hold on to stereotypes. This can be seen in ethnic minority groups that face personal and systemic racism as well as in populations such as the deaf or the blind. Assumptions about intelligence or social capacity are detrimental to self-esteem and identity formation.

Finally, educational delays can be a developmental issue contributing to emotional problems in adulthood. Learning disabilities, being kept behind in school, and poor grades are all more subtle problems. When you were walking down the school hallway, others who did not know you had no idea of your struggles. Yet your teachers and the classmates with whom you spent the most time may have formed a less favorable view of you based on your poor performance. Internally, you may have felt "dumb" when in reality your learning style may simply have differed from what was expected in the classroom environment.

If you have struggled with low self-esteem or simply feeling bad about yourself, you probably had some type of developmental issue such as those just described. You may continue even now to have negative thoughts go through your mind multiple times every day. Therapists have referred to these as "old tapes" (though perhaps we should call them "repeat tracks" to keep up with technology!). Some of these messages (like, "You are so stupid," or "Why can't you just get with it") play in your mind over and over, continually reinforcing the ideas formed in childhood.

## ABUSE

Another problem from the past that can haunt a person throughout life is that of abuse. There are many types of abuse, including verbal, emotional, physical, and sexual. Abuse can happen to anyone at any time, from children to the elderly and anyone in between. As we discuss abuse, we will specifically be talking about abuse at the hands of someone you know. Rape, kidnapping, or other abuses at the hand of a stranger fall into the category of trauma that we will discuss in the next section.

Let's begin by discussing verbal abuse. This term may sound vague and may be hard to define, but generally speaking verbal abuse is ongoing derogatory and/or insulting speech intended to maintain emotional control over another person. We all have bad days, and when your spouse occasionally snaps at you it is not verbal abuse. A pattern of demeaning another person is abusive because it keeps the relationship imbalanced. The abuser maintains control and the victim begins to believe that he or she is truly worthless. It is important to note that both men and women can be victims of verbal abuse.

Emotional abuse is similar, but rather than the primary mode of abuse being spoken words, it is manipulative actions that are present. Withholding love, twisting reality to continually blame the other person, and passive-aggressive behavior are all forms of emotional abuse. For example, your parent, spouse, or friend may begin to sulk or act hurt when you will not give in to what they want. Payback gestures, such as "forgetting" to give you a promised ride or standing you up for a date, may be the result if you have said or done something that the person finds offensive. Sometimes you may not know what you did to trigger such a response.

Again it is important to note that we are talking about pervasive patterns that define the relationship. All relationships have conflict, and sometimes when we are at our worst we do not handle it well. When these behaviors I am describing happen occasionally, it does not signal abuse. When emotional abuse is occurring, *most* interactions involve manipulation. It is the norm rather than a resolvable conflict.

Physical abuse is another form of abuse that can happen from parents to children, or between spouses or partners. Any type of hitting, pushing, or even physically blocking an exit are all examples of physical abuse. A sad yet powerful story of a child's experience of physical abuse can be found in *A Child Called It* by Dave Pelzer (1995).

In the case of physical abuse, a pervasive pattern is not needed for abuse to be present. Any form of physical violence inflicted from one person to another, even just once, is never acceptable and is a crime. If you are a victim of domestic violence or know of a child who is experiencing physical abuse, you should contact police and other local authorities immediately. There are many agencies with safe houses and other services that can help you get out of an unsafe situation.

Some children bear witness to domestic violence even if they are never physically abused themselves. If you experienced this as a child, you may find yourself carrying anger with you or you may get involved in physical altercations yourself. You are likely to have a strong sense of justice, and if left unresolved this could lead you to act out your feelings in ways that may include violence. Working through the issues of your past with a Christian counselor can help you find ways to use your sense of justice productively rather than allowing violence to continue to have power in your life.

The last form of abuse we will discuss here is sexual abuse. Again, we do not need a pattern of behavior to classify unwanted or inappropriate sexual acts as abuse. One incident crosses the line to abuse and can continue to haunt a person throughout his or her life.

Sexual abuse has become more recognized as victims have bravely come forward in the past ten to twenty years to share their stories. Tragically, sometimes the perpetrators of sexual abuse are people that are in positions of power or trust, like parents, relatives, neighbors, priests, or teachers. Any type of touching on sexual areas of the body that is unwanted or perpetrated by an adult to a minor is abuse.

Secrecy is very often involved in this form of abuse. While domestic violence can sometimes be loud or alert neighbors, sexual abuse is hidden and can go on for years without anyone finding out. Abusers frequently use control tactics to threaten victims and make them afraid to come forward. Perhaps even more tragic is that some victims who do report the abuse are not believed, particularly when the abuser is someone in close relationship with the family.

If you have been sexually abused, healing is possible for you. Seek a counselor or safe person with whom you can share your story. Sometimes with this support, you develop the strength to report your abuse to authorities and prevent others from being abused as well.

## TRAUMATIC EVENTS

Abuse is certainly a traumatic event, but as we discuss various issues stemming from your past it is helpful to classify abuse and other types of traumatic events separately. Here I am referring to accidents, witnessing or experiencing a crime, war trauma, and loss. These events can lead to specific anxiety symptoms commonly known as Post-Traumatic Stress Disorder. Not everyone who experiences a trauma develops PTSD, but symptoms include avoidance of certain places or things that remind you of the trauma, a sense of re-experiencing the trauma in the form of dreams or triggers, and a hypervigilant outlook that may make you feel that you are constantly looking over your shoulder.

If you have ever been in even a small car accident, you are likely to relate to the fact that your brain stops processing correctly when a sudden, startling event occurs. I remember my first fender bender a few months after getting my driver's license. I was turning left in a large intersection that had two left turn lanes. I had not had experience in that scenario and did not manage to stay in my lane while making the turn. Can I tell you exactly what happened? No. I was not physically hurt and the accident was minor. But the moment something went wrong I was confused, startled, and I had no idea how the accident had happened. Afterwards I could piece together events in my mind and see where I must have gone wrong, but I did not have any actual memories of leaving my lane. I did not bump my head or have any physical reason for a disrupted memory, but the sudden shock had caused my brain to stop processing normally.

Our brains are designed to use three types of memory: working, short-term, and long-term. Working memory helps you add numbers in your head or remember an address until you can grab a paper to write it down. These memories do not get stored by your brain because they are only needed for a short time. Once you are done with the information it is discarded.

Short-term memory can last for perhaps a day or even a week or so. Where you parked your car five hours ago when you arrived at the shopping mall is stored in short-term memory. (Though we've all probably experienced our brains discarding that information a bit too soon as we wander the parking garage aimlessly!) Events like what you ate for dinner the past three nights or which bills you need to pay next week are also short-term memory. Once time has passed or the memory is no longer needed, it is also discarded.

Some memories make it into long-term memory. These are events that stand out for some reason—perhaps a special night out, a vacation, or an unusual conversation. Our brains catalog these for later recall, and while we are able to recall long-term memories at will, they do not stay in our awareness.

Trauma interrupts the brain's cataloguing efforts. Instead of a short-term memory (an event that happened today) getting processed into long-term memory, it gets stuck in short-term memory. Because trauma is startling and stimulates fear, the brain has trouble marking such an event as "resolved." Thus, after a trauma occurs, you may feel like you are reliving the experience as if it is actually happening. This phenomenon is directly a result of being stuck in short-term memory.

Witnessing a crime, being a victim of crime such as kidnapping or rape, or being a soldier at war all cause the brain to get interrupted as it does with accidents. Loss, however, can be slightly different depending on the type of loss and how it occurred. A sudden loss connected with an accident, crime, or war will likely still have the brain processing issues I described. Loss such as the death of a spouse may not follow quite the same pattern.

Grief and trauma have many similarities,

but it is important to make some distinctions. In both grief and trauma the brain has trouble resolving feelings connected with the loss. However, grief does not often have the symptoms associated with PTSD. Fear of another loss may be present, but you are less likely to be hypervigilant or startled in the same way as someone who has experienced a sudden, shocking event.

Dr. Elisabeth Kubler-Ross created the now famous five-stage model of grief in 1969. She asserted that there are five distinct stages that those who are grieving work through: denial, anger, bargaining, depression, and acceptance.[9] One who is grieving does not necessarily move through these stages in a direct order, and may find that stages are repeated.

If you have experienced loss in your life, it is important to allow yourself time to grieve. In my years as a counselor, I cannot recall one person going through grief who did not feel as though they should be "over it by now." We often want to rush grief, or we put expectations on ourselves that limit the "acceptable" amount of time to grieve. Grief is a very personal process, and one in which you can find healing as you work through your feelings. Allow your feelings

---

[9] *On Death and Dying.* New York: Scribner.

to come and go as they will, keeping yourself grounded in your relationship with God and with others who can support you.

## PAST MISTAKES

Every human being has made mistakes. You have sinned, you have made errors that were purely accidental, and you have taken paths that in hindsight were perhaps not the best. We all have regrets, but for some of us our regrets and feelings of guilt haunt us and stop us from being able to move forward emotionally and spiritually.

There are a few different types of regrets we will highlight here: harmful relationships, missed opportunities, poor choices, and crimes committed. I am sure that some of you will have examples of regrets that do not fall into these categories, but for the most part these categories cover common types of regrets.

Harmful relationships can create intense pain that lasts for many years past the end of the relationship. In our chapter on relationships, many types of harmful relationships were described. If you have experienced these, you may experience regret and you may question yourself. "How could I have stayed in the relationship as long as I did?" Or perhaps, "How could I have treated another person so badly?"

Often when you have harmed others, by the time you are able to look back and realize what you have done, the relationship is badly damaged and the other person may be unwilling to give you another chance. These ongoing consequences are a painful reality for many.

Missed opportunities can also have us kicking ourselves for years if we allow them to take hold. The nagging, "If only..." is something that makes us want to run back into our past and change our minds. The feeling of wanting to change the past can cause despair, and it also paralyzes us in the present. When we focus on what we cannot control, we miss present opportunities to live differently.

Our own poor choices can also wreak havoc on our present emotional health as we punish ourselves for our bad decisions. For instance, addictions that have torn families apart leave those in recovery feeling a deep sense of loss and regret over the poor choices they made. There is a sad cost that is still being paid. Living with the present consequences of past mistakes can be a maddening experience as you seek to move forward in your life. Illness brought on by our poor choices, lost relationships, or financial ruin that continues to harm us daily are a reminder of a life we once lived.

If you have ever committed a crime,

whether convicted or not, you may feel like receiving God's forgiveness is emotionally impossible. People stuck in this past issue can struggle with really believing that God can forgive what they have done. Some types of violent crimes or patterns of criminal activity work their way into your understanding of yourself. You may identify yourself as a murderer, abuser, or thief. You may, in the deepest places of your brokenness, believe that you are too "bad" to be worth forgiving.

## HEALING FROM YOUR PAST

No matter what has happened in your past, I firmly believe that healing is available to you. Jesus came to the earth for the broken, the hurting, the ones whose lives were full of pain and regret. The hope offered in the Bible is available to you, and if you have not read the Bible, you should explore its pages. The gospel of Mark is a great place to start to just get to know Jesus and the kinds of people He came to rescue.

Those facing issues from the past have lost their sense of self. Their identity is so far from what God created them to be that they are almost unrecognizable. Questions about God can also be really complicated as you may wonder where God was when you were experiencing abuse, trauma, or loss. These questions often do not have direct answers, but we do need to recognize the power of Satan in the world. The Bible describes Satan as a thief and a liar. He seeks to destroy us and then convinces us to blame God for what he has done. When we recognize the spiritual realities around us, we begin to understand the character of God and the ways in which He is ready to redeem and restore us. We can enter into the battle and fight for our own healing.

Issues of the past not only rob us of our identity, but they also create fear, shame, and guilt feelings that have potential to rule our minds. These feelings fester and multiply when we keep them to ourselves. Honesty is a key to healing. When you share your story including these deepest feelings of fear, shame, and guilt with a trusted counselor, pastor, or friend, you are no longer alone. Trust may be a challenge for you, but you cannot heal alone. The weight of your past is too big for you to carry by yourself.

## NEXT STEPS

No matter what has happened in your past, it is over. You are in a new moment, with a new chance to live well. Below are some ways you can begin your healing journey:

**Write or tell your story.** In cases of abuse or

traumatic events, you were powerless and victimized. Finding your voice as someone who has experienced a difficult past is powerful in the healing process. Sharing your story on your terms can give you a sense of empowerment and can help you process all that has happened.

> *Psalm 31:17*—Don't let me be disgraced, O LORD, for I call out to you for help. Let the wicked be disgraced; let them lie silent in the grave.

**Explore forgiveness.** Forgiveness helps you. It is not about ignoring a wrong—just the opposite! It acknowledges the severity of the wrong done to you or done by you and gives you a choice to no longer allow it to have power over you. Forgiveness does not happen in one day. Take your time and release any bitterness, anger, shame, or guilt you still carry.

> *Matthew 6:12*—And forgive us our sins, as we have forgiven those who sin against us.

**Re-define your identity.** You are not who you once were. You are no longer abused, you are no longer an abuser. You do not live in your past and you are strong and resilient. God is able to transform you into someone new. Define yourself in Christ.

> *Galatians 4:7*—Now you are no longer a slave but God's own child. And since you are his child, God has made you his heir.

**Renew your mind.** Practice a lifestyle of mindfulness, being aware of each moment you are in. Pay attention to your present—the smells, sounds, and sights that surround you now. Contrast these new realities with your past to remind yourself that you are no longer in the place you have been.

> *John 14:27*—'I am leaving you with a gift—peace of mind and heart. And the peace I give is a gift the world cannot give. So don't be troubled or afraid.'

**Fight the battle.** We are in a very real spiritual war with a real enemy. Satan has caused the pain in your life and has trapped you with his lies. Keeping this battle in mind can help you fight for freedom in the midst of everyday life.

> *1 Peter 5:8*—Stay alert! Watch out for your great enemy, the devil. He prowls around like a roaring lion, looking for

someone to devour.

**Become an advocate.** Helping others who may face similar circumstances to your own can be a powerful way to find healing and make a difference. Volunteer, become a mentor, or share your story publicly. Give back and help others face their pasts as well. In the Bible, Joseph is a good example of someone who healed from a traumatic past, forgave his family, and was able to become a prominent leader.

> *Genesis 45:3-8*—"I am Joseph!" he said to his brothers. "Is my father still alive?" But his brothers were speechless! They were stunned to realize that Joseph was standing there in front of them. "Please, come closer," he said to them. So they came closer. And he said again, "I am Joseph, your brother, whom you sold into slavery in Egypt. But don't be upset, and don't be angry with yourselves for selling me to this place. It was God who sent me here ahead of you to preserve your lives. This famine that has ravaged the land for two years will last five more years, and there will be neither plowing nor harvesting. God has sent me ahead of you to keep you and your families alive and to

preserve many survivors. So it was God who sent me here, not you! And he is the one who made me an adviser to Pharaoh—the manager of his entire palace and the governor of all Egypt.

# 6

## SELF-CARE: WHY HEALTHY HABITS MATTER

Most Christians could quote the verse, "Love your neighbor as yourself." Ironically, not everyone is so good at actually loving themselves. How well you take care of yourself is a reflection on your internal state: do you care about yourself? Before we talk about routines and habits, we need to first figure out how you feel about yourself. Are you worth taking care of?

When I led a workshop based on my previous book, *Getting Your Life Under Control,* I made a comment about pairing new habits with old ones. I stated a basic assumption that everyone brushes their teeth, and I suggested that people establish one new habit linked to tooth-brushing. If you want to read your Bible more, for example, put it in the bathroom under your toothbrush so that you see it when you brush your teeth and can establish the habit of reading your Bible at that time.

Do you know what I learned from that suggestion? Many people do not brush their teeth regularly! I had several people tell me in the weeks following the workshop that they had begun to brush their teeth since I mentioned it at the workshop.

If you are not able to meet your basic needs like tooth-brushing, what does it mean to love your neighbor as yourself? If you do not love yourself and you do not take care of yourself, you will be ineffective in ministry and your ability to influence others will be limited. You may be able to serve others or offer encouragement, but when people take a look at how you take care of your physical body, your home, and your life they may wonder whether or not they can rely on your influence.

You might argue with me at this point: "I brush my teeth and shower every day. I present well. So what if I don't eat well or exercise? What does that matter to my spiritual life?" Sadly, even many pastors fall into the category of people with poor self-care. Perhaps they are the perfect example of why self-care is important: your ministry will be cut short and your effectiveness limited if you are not an example of health to others. Many pastors are at high risk for heart attack or stroke because of being overweight and taking on too much stress. They may feel they are helping others now and justify putting their ministry ahead of their own self-care. But if they develop serious health problems, their very lives may be at stake. If your body is truly the dwelling place of God, surely taking care of it (or not) must have an impact on your spiritual life.

In this chapter we are not going to focus on the practical elements of self-care. There are many suggestions in my previous book mentioned earlier that you can draw from. Rather, here we will discuss four key reasons *why* people do not have good self-care habits: *inattention, overachievement, lack of motivation,* and *avoidance.* We will also take a look at the impact of these patterns on your overall life and health, and I will offer suggestions for systemic change in the *Next Steps* section at the end of the chapter.

## INATTENTION

Let's begin with the most basic way people neglect self-care: inattention. This simply means that a person is ignorant or unaware of his or her needs or does not understand why self-care is important. The inattentive person does not intend to neglect self-care, nor is he aware of doing so. Most likely the inattentive person did not have good adult models of self-care. Perhaps hygiene standards were low or exercise/nutrition habits were never taught.

For the inattentive type, there are some problems that will surface. Generally, physical needs will be met inconsistently, leading to confusion and disorder in the body. Sleep is likely to be inconsistent. If you find yourself going to bed at different times every night and waking up at different times every morning, you may fall into the inattentive category. If someone asked you if you sleep well, you might say "yes" because your sleep is not interrupted. However, your body is likely to be experiencing affects you aren't even noticing, such as fluctuating moods or fatigue.

When inattention is the cause of a lack of self-care, nutrition is also likely to be affected. You may be totally unaware of how many calories you are consuming, whether or not you are getting adequate nutrients, or whether or not you are gaining or losing weight. Eventually you will notice these results, usually in a surprising wake-up-call moment when you suddenly realize you are 30 pounds heavier or you have developed a health problem.

Exercise is virtually non-existent for the

inattentive type. If you exercise less than twelve times per year and do not think about exercise in between these moments, you are inattentive to your body's needs. Without exercise, you increase your risk of heart problems, stroke, and many other physical complications. Our bodies were designed for physical labor, a rare description for most jobs in America. Unless you are plowing a field all day, you are probably not getting the physical activity you need from your regular activities. Even if you don't need to lose weight, exercise is essential to your overall long-term health and your emotional balance.

The key to combatting inattention is *awareness*. Ask your doctor or do some research to find out how much sleep and exercise you need. Explore nutrition, including how much water you should take in daily. Once you have become aware of these needs, pay attention to how your body feels when its needs are met versus when they are not.

### OVERACHIEVEMENT

Many Americans probably fall into the category of overachievement. Our entire culture centers on climbing the ladder, pulling yourself up by your own bootstraps, and being productive as a demonstration of your worth. Especially in tougher economic times, Americans work more for less money. Some do not take vacation time given to them for fear of being replaced by someone more dedicated. Some work hourly, low-wage jobs and do not get paid if they take any time off. Working while sick is not only commonplace, but it's often expected or financially necessary.

Regardless of socioeconomic or career status, most Americans would be likely to describe themselves as "busy." I have asked people who do not work at all as well as people who work 80 hours per week to tell me how their week has been. "Oh, busy..." is almost always the answer. Those who are not busy inevitably feel that they *should* be busy, and they believe their lack of busyness is a problem.

You don't have to feel like you are getting ahead in life to be an overachiever. Simply have a "busy" life is all it takes to feel you have no time for self-care. You might be a like a cat chasing your tail, running in circles with absolutely no real gain, yet you neglect self-care because you are too busy. Unlike the inattentive type, you may be aware that you are not slowing down or taking care of yourself. You are more likely to feel guilty for not eating right or exercising, yet you don't make time for these habits either. *Should* is your operative word.

Your life will be impacted by your lack of

self-care. In the area of sleep, those who are overachievers will be likely not to get enough sleep. Whereas the inattentive types had inconsistent sleep, you may have a regular bedtime and wake-time. But you may not be budgeting enough sleep time, scraping by with 6-7 hours per night when you really need 8-9. You may find that you would say your bedtime is 10pm, when really you are consistently still puttering around until 11pm. Your bedtime is consistent, but it is not what you claim it to be.

Those who are overachievers are also impacted in their eating habits. If you fall into this category, you may find that you inadvertently skip meals or eat meals on the go because you are rushing. If "multi-tasking" is your middle name, keep a food journal for a week. How often are you simply not eating, or eating while doing other tasks?

Your digestion and quality of food intake will be affected by rushing eating or eating on the go. You will not enjoy eating and you may be eating foods with high sugar or sodium levels that come pre-packaged. Your stress level is also likely to be high, so ulcers or gastrointestinal problems are potential issues for you.

Finally, your ability to exercise will continually be met with the excuse, "I don't have time..." Most of us are wasting time without being aware of doing so. Track your activities for a week to see how much TV you are watching or how much time you spend on Facebook or surfing the web. When you value something, you make time for it. So the question you must ask is this: why do I place a low value on exercise? Determine what specific benefits exercise can bring to your life, physically and emotionally, and find ways to set other things aside or fill time that has been spent on activities that have been fruitless in your life.

The main principle for change for those who overachieve is *slow down*. Your constant busyness is not healthy, and it is probably not helping you or others nearly as much as you think. Sadly, because our culture ties worth and value to our level of productivity and busyness, we may believe that if we slow down we are weak or unimportant. Jesus did not demonstrate a frantic, hurried way of life. He took time apart from the crowds despite the fact that this surely meant some people did not receive His help. Realizing your own limitations and slowing down your pace of life are critical to regulating your emotions and preventing disease. Don't sprint until you crash… Slow and steady wins the race.

## LACK OF MOTIVATION

Others may find themselves aware of their needs with plenty of time to spare. Yet there is still a neglect of self-care. If this sounds like you, you may have a lack of motivation. Depression is a common cause for decreased motivation as well as for generally poor self-esteem. You may struggle to get out of bed in the morning, or you may have daily self-defeating thoughts like, "Why bother?" or "Nothing I do really matters anyway." Or you may simply just not feel like doing it.

For those who lack motivation, sleep can be affected in that you are probably getting too much sleep or you may struggle with insomnia. These are specific symptoms of depression. Your body's rhythms are off and self-care is the key to getting this back on track. This includes talking with your doctor about safe medications that can improve your mood and help you sleep.

Food intake may be high for those with a lack of motivation. You might eat in order to cope, finding emotional comfort in food. When you think about eating healthy, that "Why bother?" attitude may come out when you are faced with feelings of sadness or discontent. Again, keeping a food journal can help you track your intake. Add a spot in your charting for a mood rating: each time you eat, is your mood a

"1" (extremely sad or depressed) or a "10" (the best you've ever felt) or somewhere in between? Making the connection between your eating and your emotions can help pinpoint triggers. Finding other coping skills to manage your feelings is essential to getting your eating under control.

Exercise is absolutely essential for anyone struggling with a lack of motivation. Unfortunately, it also can be hardest for those who with depression or low self-esteem to get moving. Interrupting this cycle is possible. Making sure you have explored your options for medication may help combat the depression enough to get you to a place where you can begin to exercise. If you want to avoid medication, then exercise is the number one way to do that. Various studies have shown that exercise can be as effective in treating depression as a low dose of an anti-depressant.

Another way to break the cycle is to make exercise easy. Joining a gym may feel like an obstacle too great to overcome, or your poor self-esteem may make you feel self-conscious around others who are also working out. Just getting outside to take a walk around the block is a good start. Don't set goals for weight loss or put pressure on yourself to achieve. Simply get moving in a way that is as easy as possible.

Jumping rope, doing sit ups, walking, using fitness video games, or jumping on a trampoline may be easier than other forms of exercise. If you need extra support, ask a friend to walk with you or keep you accountable.

Understanding the root causes of your negative sense of self or depressed mood is critical if you are going to improve your self-care. Of all the categories I am describing in this chapter, you may be the most skeptical about the need for self-care. Until your beliefs about yourself change, you will be stuck emotionally and spiritually. If you have even a tiny amount of hope that your life could get better than it is right now, use that faith to venture into self-care. Once you begin to take care of yourself, you will continually find it easier to keep going.

## AVOIDANCE

The final reason for a lack of self-care is avoidance. Those who fall into this category tend to feel a sense of fear or anxiety, and they may make excuses when it comes to self-care. Perhaps you have felt a fear of failure: "If I exercise but don't lose weight I'll feel worse than I do now," or "If I go to the doctor or start taking care of myself I'll find out I've already developed high blood pressure or diabetes." Most often these types of fears are irrational—you know rationally that it makes more sense to take care of yourself to avoid the realization of your fears, yet your fear overrides rationality and you are immobilized.

For those in this group, sleep is likely to be affected by racing thoughts or frequent waking. Continual worry may keep you up at night or wake you up in the middle of the night. You may even have bad dreams that tie in to the fears or anxiety you feel when awake.

In the area of nutrition, you may have an all-or-nothing approach. You may try to restrict your eating for a while, or overeat when nervous. A pattern of binging, purging, or starving yourself may tie in to the root issues causing your fear in the first place. Your weight may yo-yo as you try crash diets—these are not self-care but rather an attempt to feel in control of an area in which you fear being out of control. You avoid a balanced approach to self-care out of fear that you will become overweight or that self-care won't really make you feel any better.

Exercise is similarly affected, as you make excuses for why exercising is too hard for you or why you cannot exercise in moderation. You may alternate periods of intense exercise with periods of no exercise at all. When you do start an exercise routine, you may give up quickly when you don't get results.

For those of you who see yourself in this *avoidance* category, your primary focus is facing your fears. You may want to explore with a Christian counselor what your fears are and where they come from. If you are making excuses to avoid taking care of yourself, identify what those excuses are and then try to figure out the fear underneath that excuse. Then you can ask yourself, "What if..." and imagine the worst-case scenario if your fear occurred. What if you found out you had a medical disorder? What if you exercised but didn't lose weight? Try to find the positive outcomes, such as, "I could get proper treatment if I was diagnosed," or "I will get mental benefits from exercise regardless of any weight loss."

Most fear is irrational. You will not be fully able to talk yourself into rationally getting rid of it. As you ask, "What if..." you are engaging your emotions and allowing yourself to feel the feeling. If you have a specific fear you can begin to slowly and gradually expose yourself to it in order to decrease the fear response. When you begin to practice self-care and your feared scenarios do not play out, you will start to let go of the fear. I know, now you are thinking, "But what if my fears DO come true??!!" The only way to know is to slowly walk towards it to find out.

## FINDING BALANCE

Regardless of the underlying reason, anyone who has not been practicing self-care is not able to respond to stress well. Life happens. Stress happens. Your responses to stress will be unhelpful if you have very little margin in your life. We all need a little emotional wiggle-room so that when stress comes we are not pushed over the edge. Self-care creates that wiggle-room.

I have asked some of my clients to imagine calling 9-1-1 to request an ambulance and getting a frantic, stressed EMT arriving at the door. We realize that an emergency responder must remain calm in order to successfully manage the crisis situation. Yet we respond to our own lives in a frenzied panic when we do not practice self-care. We are ineffective and we are unable to move forward emotionally and spiritually.

Good self-care promotes a balanced life in which you properly understand yourself, your limitations, and your needs. Acknowledging that you are worth taking care of and noticing your body's sleep, nutritional, and exercise needs are essential for a sense of balance. This concept is counter-cultural—to get ahead we are encouraged to work harder or push ourselves. Last time I was sick, my cough drop gave me a pep-talk with a message on the wrapper to "power through." No! Get rest, take care of yourself, give yourself permission to slow down.

Spiritually, self-care helps you understand your place in relationship with God: humble, human, imperfect, and loved. We are free to love ourselves because God loves us. We are able to declare our worth and value because He has chosen to give us value. Humbly understanding yourself—viewing yourself the way God views you—is a part of the fear of God. His power is made perfect in our weakness, yet at the same time He chose to save us and place us at His right hand.

## NEXT STEPS

There are many steps you can take to improve your self-care. Here are some concrete ways you can get started:

**Identify your baseline.** Your baseline self-care behavior is your current activity level. Do you exercise once per week? Do you eat fast food every day for lunch? These actions represent the baseline, or beginning, prior to change. Understanding your baseline is important for the creation of realistic goals. You are unlikely to succeed if you set a goal to run a marathon next week when your baseline behavior has been no exercise for the past six months. Accept your baseline as your starting point, even if you feel ashamed of your current state. Avoid beating yourself up; instead, encourage yourself for the steps you are taking to move out of that negative place now.

> *Romans 12:3-5*—Because of the privilege and authority God has given me, I give each of you this warning: Don't think you are better than you really are. Be honest in your evaluation of yourselves, measuring yourselves by the faith God has given us. Just as our bodies have many parts and each part has a special function, so it is with Christ's body. We are many parts of one body, and we all belong to each other.

**Make a list of daily physical needs.** Most adults need 7-9 hours of sleep per night, 3-5 periods of moderate exercise weekly, daily social interaction, a healthy diet comprised of mostly unprocessed foods, work periods, and rest periods. You may have these and/or other physical needs. When you prioritize and meet these needs, you give yourself the best chance to feel emotional balance and wellness. Create your own daily checklist, and if you feel off-balance use the list as a guide to be sure you have not neglected self-care.

> *1 Corinthians 6:19-20*—Don't you realize that your body is the temple of the Holy Spirit, who lives in you and was given to you by God? You do not belong to yourself, for God bought you with a high price. So you must honor God with your body.

**Start with the easiest need**. It is tempting to challenge yourself to conquer a difficult goal when you feel a desire for change. Resist the temptation to achieve your hardest goal first. As we discussed earlier regarding identifying your baseline, you should make one small change that is not very far from your current behavior. When you feel the success of making a small change, you are likely to build on that success. Starting with a big change or multiple changes at once is more likely to end in failure.

> *1 Corinthians 9:26-27*—So I run with purpose in every step. I am not just shadowboxing. I discipline my body like an athlete, training it to do what it should. Otherwise, I fear that after preaching to others I myself might be disqualified.

**Encourage yourself.** Encouraging yourself simply reflects the truth about who you are in Christ. I am not suggesting that you soothe yourself with empty words or tell yourself, "Everything is fine," when in fact there are problems in your life. Rather, use the truth: you are loved by God, you are worth taking care of, you want to move forward in life. Making true, positive statements can help counter the many negative thoughts that may be running through your mind. Be kind to yourself.

*Colossians 3:12*—Since God chose you to be the holy people he loves, you must clothe yourselves with tenderhearted mercy, kindness, humility, gentleness, and patience.

**Value yourself.** Valuing yourself goes deeper than just encouragement. Your sense of self runs to the deepest core of your being. Take time to write down your strengths and weaknesses. Do you tend to focus on the negative? What thoughts go through your mind when you look at yourself in the mirror? What experiences have shaped your understanding of yourself? Take time to connect with yourself and with God to more deeply explore who you believe you are and who God has made you to be.

*Galatians 4:7*—Now you are no longer a slave but God's own child. And since you are his child, God has made you his heir.

# 7

## MOVING FORWARD

Discipleship is the process of becoming more like Christ. Emotionally and spiritually, we follow Jesus' example and seek the freedom He offers. Being a Christian is not about getting a ticket to Heaven, or having a spiritual insurance policy. It is about total surrender—giving up everything in obedience to God.

As we have explored emotional health and its connection to your spiritual growth, we have looked at a variety of areas that can hold you back. We will now turn our focus to *moving forward* as disciples of Christ. If you identified traps in your thinking, relationships, addictive behaviors, past, or self-care, you need to decide whether or not you believe you can live in freedom. And you need to form a picture in your mind about what that freedom might look like.

Moving forward is not about becoming a "better Christian" on the outside. It is not about ignoring symptoms of a mental health disorder or blaming yourself for not having "enough" faith. It is about taking stock of where you are and figuring out what your "next level" would look like. Let's walk through specifically how to *accept where you are, understand your identity, recognize the enemy,* and *use strategic tools* to move forward in your discipleship process.

## ACCEPT WHERE YOU ARE

During more than a decade working in the mental health field, I have often seen people beat themselves up emotionally when they gain insight into problems in their lives. Through the counseling process, people often realize things about themselves that they had not known. Perhaps as you have read this book you identified emotional traps you are in, and you may now find yourself thinking, "How could you not see this? How could you let this happen? You are more screwed up than you even thought you were before..."

Tearing yourself down is the exact opposite of what you need in this moment. I have compared this to running a marathon and tripping yourself along the way. You are already dealing with enough emotional turmoil. Don't add to the pile by berating yourself about it. Instead, be kind and encouraging to yourself as you move through the process of change.

So exactly how do you go about accepting where you are? What if you don't like where you are? What if you feel horrible and cannot bring yourself to accept that this is the way life is for you? You start by accepting yourself as a dynamic being designed to grow and change. If you were to break your leg, you would understand instinctively that with proper help your leg will heal. You would not say, "I will not accept the fact that my leg is broken. I cannot live the rest of my life with a broken leg!" In accepting yourself in your current circumstances, you are not declaring that life will *always* be this way. You are accepting that *right now* you will no longer deny or ignore the problems you have uncovered.

When you have committed to being kind and encouraging to yourself and have accepted where you are right now, you can begin to heal. Being realistic is critical to change. What are you ready for right now? How can you create goals, prioritize, and take one step at a time? In *Getting Your Life Under Control* I have answered these questions in detail and would encourage you to read that book to make a plan for moving forward.

## UNDERSTAND YOUR IDENTITY

In addition to accepting where you are right now, you need to start to understand yourself in a whole new light. Your identity is not defined by the problems you face. If you have pervasive negative thinking, a pattern of chaotic relationships, a life-controlling addiction, a troubled past, or difficulty caring for yourself, your identity is not those things. Your identity is not a label: depressed, chaotic, anxious, addicted, victimized, or lazy. These are not qualities that reflect God's character, and since the Bible tells us that we are made in the image of God we know that He did not design us to be identified as such.

It only took two chapters of the Bible for a perfect world to unravel. By chapter 3, mankind had chosen an act of disobedience with catastrophic consequences. The labels I listed above are part of living in a sin-cursed world. While we must seek to recognize sin issues in our own lives, much of what I have described in this book is not a result of anything you have done. Our bodies, our minds, and our environments are damaged.

You are not your problems. You are a beautiful and wonderful creation of God— someone He loves deeply and values enough to send His Son to earth to save. When He looks at you, He does not see your issues as who you are. He sees these broken places as something to redeem and restore. If you have never given your life to God and asked Him to rescue you, I would invite you to do that right now. All you have to do is ask. Then you can turn to the Bible and a local church to help you understand who Jesus is and how to be like Him.

If you have given your life to Christ and continue to experience emotional traps, you are not alone. Becoming a Christian does not instantly remove every problem from your life. In fact, sometimes you become more aware of problems that you were previously ignoring. As I have said, being a "good Christian" does not mean you have it all together. It means seeking God no matter where you find yourself. It means obedience, trust, and perseverance. And sometimes it means finding connection with God in the midst of suffering. Jesus' suffering on earth and His victory means that we always have hope that He has something better for our future.

## RECOGNIZE THE ENEMY

The Bible describes a very real enemy of God that is constantly at work to destroy our lives. He made his appearance in that third chapter of Genesis and he has not stopped seeking to keep us far from God. When you have identified emotional traps, remember that these snares were put in your life by Satan. He wants to keep you ensnared and enslaved, and even more he wants you to think it is your fault and inherent to who you are.

At my church we have a saying that frequently comes up: Satan is a liar. We continually remind ourselves of this truth because it is so easy to forget. In our rational, logical society, talking about Satan and lies you believe can make you feel a little crazy sometimes. And yet denying this spiritual reality is even crazier because it is really quite obvious when you stop to pay attention.

You are not your enemy. So stop fighting yourself. When you have identified emotional traps or problematic thinking, recognize these as the work of Satan in your life. Ephesians 6:12 says,

> For we are not fighting against flesh-and-blood enemies, but against evil rulers and authorities of the unseen world, against mighty powers in this dark world, and against evil spirits in the heavenly places.

Every negative thought you have is part of the way Satan is attacking you to keep you from moving forward. Every addiction is a tool of the enemy to keep you far from obedience to God.

C.S. Lewis' book *The Screwtape Letters* is a humorous look inside the demonic world. A more experienced demon writes to an apprentice about various "good ideas" for tricking and trapping humans. From alluring women to self-doubt, there are a host of ways the demons mess with the minds of men.[10] If you want to begin to think through some ways Satan may try to trap you, that book might be a good start.

You cannot fight an enemy that you do not recognize. You must know his strategies and be on guard. It is also critical to know where you are weak—where is he most likely to attack? Whatever traps you have identified as you have read this book are likely targets that Satan has hit over and over in your life. Your awareness of those issues, and your understanding of those issues as not linked to your identity, can help you fight off these attacks in a new way.

If you identify yourself by your problems, you cannot combat what you feel will never be removed from you. But if you recognize your true enemy and have faith that you do not have to live this way forever, you can battle your way into freedom. Any step you take towards

[10] Lewis, C.S. (2009). *The Screwtape Letters* (Reprint ed.). San Fransisco: HarperOne.

wellness is an advance on the battle lines. Whether it is praying, going to counseling, exercising, taking medication, filling your mind with the truth of the Bible, or going to a recovery group, your pursuit of health and freedom fights the work of Satan. Battle is hard, and there will certainly be times you feel you are defeated or you cannot go on. Do not battle alone—ask others to encourage you and pray for you, and develop a support network of pastors, mentors, counselors, and friends.

## USE STRATEGIC TOOLS

All of the wellness steps I just listed are part of your strategic toolbox. The pursuit of emotional health requires work and requires strategy. You will not accidentally get better. You will have to force yourself at times to push through even when you feel like giving up. But if you regularly use strategic tools you will be able to fight the battle more easily and effectively.

There are different types of strategic tools. Some are habits that you need every day, like getting enough sleep, eating healthy foods, or connecting with friends. But sometimes emotional traps or mental disorders prevent you from success in even meeting these daily needs. For example, self-care is a strategic tool, but if you are trapped in one of the ways I described in chapter 6, then you need different tools in order to get yourself to a place in which you can begin to develop some of these habits. Understanding the exact nature of your problems will help you develop personalized tools.

Self-observation and journaling are two key strategic tools that can help pry open the trap you are in. Self-observation is simply stepping outside yourself in order to watch your own thinking, feelings, and behavior. One of the analogies I have used with almost all of my clients describes self-observation. Imagine you are going to a movie at the theater. If it is a good movie, you will probably strongly identify with the main character or otherwise feel "sucked in" to the movie. When I am at the theater and the lights come on after the movie has finished, I often find myself a little dazed, and I have to come back to reality. A movie critic, on the other hand, goes to a movie and remains an objective observer. He does not get immersed in the plot, but rather he observes details such as camera angle, music, or acting quality. He remains in his reality the whole time and by the end is not in a fog.

Self-observation involves treating your life like a movie for which you are a movie critic. You can step back and be an observer, not allowing your thinking or feelings to suck you in but watching your reactions and evaluating them. This skill takes time to develop. To get started, simply begin once per day rating your mood on a scale from 1 to 10. Write down your rating on a calendar and when you have done this seven days in a row, start rating yourself twice a day, morning and night. You can then begin to notice trends in your rating, and perhaps start writing down other helpful information such as events that happened just prior to your mood getting better or worse.

You can also start observing yourself in relationships, notice triggers or events that cause addiction relapse or anxiety tied to trauma, or become aware of your reasons for giving up on self-care. A journal is a great place to store all of these observations as you gather data that can be very valuable when you seek counseling or try to make changes. If you are not a writer, you can still journal. Don't write an essay—just jot down the date, your mood rating, and a list of any events that made your mood better or worse.

When you journal you can also explore some of your feelings. Again this can be done by making lists rather than writing an essay. I encourage my clients to begin by asking a question, such as, "What feelings do I have right now?" Then you can simply list every feeling-word that comes to mind. Be careful not to evaluate or eliminate words; just write everything that comes to mind no matter if it seems right or wrong. When you have made your list, circle the top 3 feelings. Then you can explore these feelings by asking another question, such as, "What words come to mind when I look at the word 'angry'?" Again, brainstorm every word that comes into your mind regardless of whether or not you think it makes sense right away.

When you become experienced in self-observation and journaling, you will be able to do it quickly and naturally. You will start to notice mood changes as they happen, and you will identify common triggers that set you off. It is much easier to self-correct and get back on track when you spot triggers and red flags immediately. These strategic tools can help you stay grounded in the strength that you have as you see that you are able to fight against emotional traps.

# 8
## Counseling & Medication: Who, How, and Why

Throughout this book I have described a wide range of symptoms, some of which are commonly experienced and some of which are indicative of a more serious mental health disorder. Even in cases of diagnosable depression or anxiety, serious symptoms do not always mean lifelong symptoms. While some mental illness is chronic, other disorders occur in a single episode or period in your life. Going to counseling or taking medication for symptoms you have now does not mean you will need these treatments forever.

Some Christians have strong objections to taking medications for mental health problems. There are a few reasons for this view. First, mental health disorders still carry an unfortunate stigma and some do not believe (or do not know about) current research on brain functioning. And to be fair, research in this area is sometimes flawed, at times funded by major drug companies who will benefit from discoveries of new disorders. Even the findings of quality, objective studies have not provided the "smoking gun" of a medical diagnostic test that can confirm the presence of a specific disorder. I believe that such tests will be created within my lifetime as new research uncovers biological markers. For now, we continue to rely on subjective observation of behavior that points to biological dysfunction. Unfortunately this subjectivity causes some to reject the reality of mental health disorders and dismiss the idea of a biological basis for emotional symptoms.

Another reason some Christians do not believe in taking medications is that they worry they are simply taking an easy way out or not trusting God enough. Because the Bible does advise us against worry and encourages us to be self-controlled, we sometimes incorrectly assume that we can accomplish this completely on our own. We are all affected by sin, but when symptoms of a specific disorder become life-controlling there is more at play than sheer willpower or a sinful nature. After all, most people in this situation would stop these feelings if they could do so. Experiencing mental health problems does not make you "less spiritual" than others. It often means you have a biological dysfunction that needs regulation.

From working with hundreds of Christians who have taken medications for mental health problems, I can assure you that taking medications is very often a step of faith and requires a great deal of trust in God. Medications will not take away your problems, change your personality, or remove you from living under the curse of a sinful world. When medications work correctly, you will think thoughts like, "Wow, I feel like myself again." The reason for medication is to return you to the regulated, normal state that you felt when symptoms were not present. For those with more severe, chronic conditions, medication should ease your symptoms enough to make life more manageable.

Medication is not a quick or easy fix. Some people have to go through a trial-and-error process to find the right medication for their symptoms, and others do not find total relief from symptoms even with the right medications. There are also potential side effects that should be considered and weighed against the benefits. You also need more than just medications.

Countless studies have shown that a combination of counseling and medication is the most effective treatment for mental health disorders. Self-care, including healthy eating and exercise, is also crucial to getting well.

So how do you know if you need medication or counseling? Once you decide you do need treatment, how can you find the right kind of help? And why go through all that trouble when really it just seems like so much effort? In the remainder of this chapter, we will look at the *who, how,* and *why* of counseling and medication.

## WHO

How do you know when you need counseling or medication? When is a problem more than you can solve on your own? How do you know if you are just going through a difficult time that will pass or if you are heading towards a downward spiral? I think the first step in determining this is to consult with your doctor. He or she can evaluate your medical symptoms and give you guidance on getting treatment. You can also talk to your pastor or a friend to get their perspectives. It is hard to be objective about your own circumstances. Be honest with someone who can listen and offer insight on whether your problems can be addressed with limited intervention or whether you should seek treatment from a professional.

Another way to decide on your own whether or not you need professional counseling and/or medication is to document your symptoms. We discussed this in the previous chapter when we explored strategies for self-observation. Rate your mood on a scale of 1 to 10, up to 3 times per day for at least two weeks. If you are rating above a 5 more days than not, you should consult with a doctor or counselor who can evaluate you further.

You can also take a look at your overall functioning. Has your eating and/or sleeping become disrupted? Has your work suffered because of your symptoms, either in quality or in increased sick days? Are you fighting with yourself to get out of bed in the morning? Have you had thoughts of suicide? Have you stopped doing things you once enjoyed because of your symptoms? Do you feel like your problems are controlling your life? If you answered "yes" to any of these questions you need to seek professional help as soon as possible. In the case of suicidal thoughts, call 9-1-1 if you are in immediate danger of acting on those feelings.

## HOW

Once you have decided to seek help for your symptoms, how do you find the right kind of help for the problems you face? How do you navigate the sea of professional names and titles? I have previously written on this topic for *Wyn Magazine* and will include some of that information here. (Check out *Wyn Magazine* for free at www.wynmag.com for many more great articles on Christian mental health!)

When looking for a counselor, you might find many titles that all mean just about the same thing: counselor, therapist, psychotherapist, licensed professional counselor, licensed clinical social worker, licensed mental health counselor. Look for someone who is properly licensed in your state or country.

Even when counselors share the same exact title, not all counseling styles and methods are the same. If you want short-term therapy (10-12 sessions) focused on addressing one specific problem and you tend to be a practical thinker, cognitive behavioral therapy or brief therapy might be best for you. If you feel that you need to go in depth to explore trauma, childhood issues, or think more abstractly, you might want someone who will see you for a longer or open-ended period of time. This type of therapist will also be more likely to focus on family systems and analytical approaches.

If you are interested in exploring medication options, a doctor, psychiatrist, or psychiatric nurse would be able to evaluate you and determine if you need medication. You can talk to your primary care doctor to see if he or she will prescribe medications for your mental health symptoms or you can ask for a referral to a psychiatrist. If you start by seeking a counselor, he or she can also help you determine whether or not you should consider a medication evaluation. The counselor can also help you get in touch with a medication prescriber.

When looking for a counselor or medication provider it is also important to think about how you want to pay for treatment. If you plan to use insurance, you can ask your insurance company for a list of providers in-network or if you have a specific counselor or doctor in mind you can ask if he/she takes that type of insurance. If you have to pay out of pocket, ask if the counselor offers a sliding scale fee. Most counselors will be happy to have an initial phone or in-person consultation if you want to interview a few prior to choosing. Ask the counselor if he/she offers this; you may have to pay out-of-pocket for this initial consultation or interview.

Within the Christian counseling world, there are also many differences in perspectives on treatment. Depending on your church context, your pastor may offer some counseling or may help refer you to a Christian counselor in your area. You may hear some people call themselves "Christian counselors" while others use the term "biblical counselor." These titles can indicate variations in the type of treatment you receive, so you need to take some time to assess what kind of help you are looking for.

Asking some questions can help you decide what kind of help to pursue. Are you more comfortable talking to someone in your church, or someone outside your church? Would you prefer speaking with a man or a woman, your pastor or a licensed therapist? Do you hope to see someone for just a few sessions, or do you feel you are going to need more time to unpack all that you are feeling?

Once you know what you are most comfortable with, explore your options. If there are multiple pastors at your church and you'd like to see one of them, ask about their availability. If you prefer to see a licensed therapist, you may want to ask your pastor if there is a Christian practice nearby. If you feel your pastor is opposed to counseling that includes psychology training or does not have a referral, New Life Ministries (1-800-NEW-LIFE) and Focus on the Family maintain nationwide referral lists in the U.S.

There are also some emerging

alternatives within the realm of Christian counseling that increase the accessibility of services. Online video counseling is gaining momentum within the Christian counseling realm. If you are overseas, this may be an option if you have a connection with a counselor in the States. Another newly emerging model is one in which a church hires a licensed counselor to practice in and for the church. This is the model my pastor and I have built at our church and we are in the process of helping others learn about and adopt this model. You can read more on my blog: www.churchtherapy.com.

## WHY

Whew! Finding a counselor and/or doctor to help you sounds like a lot of work! You may feel that you simply do not have the energy to do all the legwork necessary to get help. Isn't it just easier to forget about dealing with all of this?

Easier? Yes. Better? No. Ignoring your problems or choosing to live with a life-controlling issue is only going to make it worse. Leaving depression, anxiety, or other mental health problems untreated can put you at risk for other health problems in addition to your mental health symptoms declining over time. Not getting proper help can also put you at risk for making life-altering decisions, including suicide, at a time when you are certainly not at your best self.

Your thinking, relationships, addictions, past, or difficulties with self-care do not have to overtake you. You may be struggling now, but you do not have to keep living this way. If all you can find the energy to do is set up an appointment with your doctor, then just start there. If it is easier for you to meet with your pastor, then schedule that meeting today. If you have a friend who can help make some calls for you, ask for help. While the recovery and healing process is not instant, it just takes one first step to begin. The freedom that you can experience when you no longer feel emotionally trapped is worth the effort.

You should seek help if you think you might need it because you are worth it. You are valuable, you are loved by God, and your life can be so much more. You may not understand why you have had to struggle or why your life has gone the way it has, but regardless of how your life has been impacted by this broken world it can be repaired. God can restore you, heal you, and mend your broken places. Seek Him, seek help, and seek wellness, and your life will be so much more than you can imagine it to be right now.

## FINAL THOUGHTS

I hope that this book has helped you take an honest look at your emotional health and identify traps that have you stuck. I hope that you have begun to understand the connection between your emotional and spiritual health and I pray that you find the strength and courage to seek healing and freedom.

No journey worth making is easy. The path to valuable treasure is not lightly guarded. You need strategic tools and weapons to fight for your freedom, including the support of others and proper medical or psychological treatment. Every step you take towards wellness has both physical and spiritual implications. God created us for health and He desires to restore us to freedom and wholeness. Jesus' ministry demonstrated God's heart—He had compassion and restored the hearts, souls, minds, and bodies of those who sought him. From the woman at the well to the tax collectors to the blind and lame, Jesus brought about order from disorder and health from disease.

Psalm 30:2-3 captures the experience of one who has struggled and been restored, and it is a fitting end to this book:

O LORD my God, I cried to you for help, and you restored my health. You brought me up from the grave, O LORD. You kept me from falling into the pit of death.

May God restore you, set you free from emotional traps, and rescue you from sinking deeper into grief and despair.

# APPENDIX

## EMOTIONAL TRAPS QUESTIONNAIRE

Put a checkmark next to each question that is true for you.

### Thinking:

___ 1. I often feel insecure.

___ 2. I worry what others think of me.

___ 3. Others have told me that I talk too much or "come on too strong."

___ 4. I would have a hard time listing my strengths and weaknesses.

___ 5. I am often misunderstood by others.

___ 6. I sometimes hear voices or see things others do not see.

___ 7. I have seriously thought about ways I could kill myself.

___ 8. I have very strong opinions that others don't seem to share.

___ 9. I usually do not speak my mind because I don't want to be embarrassed.

___ 10. I have a hard time understanding someone else's point of view.

___ 11. I lack goals for my life and have no idea how to achieve any goals.

___ 12. I have a history of cutting myself or harming myself in some other way.

___ 13. I think negatively about myself (such as "I'm so dumb, I'm no good") more than once per day.

___ 14. I sometimes feel worthless or hopeless.

___ 15. I feel anxious more than once per week and I do not always know why.

___ 16. I feel on top of the world and feel I can do anything.

___ 17. It feels like the world is just out to get me and I can never seem to get ahead.

___ 18. I think there is something big for my life but something is always in my way.

___ 19. There is not much I can do to change the things in my life that make me unhappy.

___ 20. I often think I am better than those around me.

## Relationships:

____ 21. I struggle to find and/or keep a job.

____ 22. I do not enjoy being with my friends and family.

____ 23. I have an argument with a friend or family member more than twice per week.

____ 24. I have fewer than two close friends with whom I can share deeply.

____ 25. I have difficulty trusting others.

____ 26. I have been hurt by a lot of people in my life.

____ 27. It is hard for me to say, "I'm sorry" when I am wrong.

____ 28. I cannot forgive others easily and sometimes hold grudges.

____ 29. In an argument, I usually back down even when I think I am right.

____ 30. I become angry quickly.

____ 31. I have yelled at someone in the past week.

____ 32. Someone is mad at me right now.

___ 33. I am mad at someone else right now.

___ 34. I feel lonely at least once per week.

___ 35. I feel anxious when I open up to others or feel vulnerable.

___ 36. Sometimes I build a "wall" to keep others from hurting me.

___ 37. I usually want to figure out who is to blame when something goes wrong.

___ 38. Other people look down on me a lot.

___ 39. Sometimes I feel as though I am invisible.

___ 40. I have a hard time making friends or feel awkward in social situations.

### Addictions:

___ 41. I have smoked at least one cigarette in the past week.

___ 42. I have had at least one alcoholic beverage in the past week.

___ 43. Other people in my life have told me I need to cut down on my drinking.

___ 44. I have a secret addiction I have never told anyone about.

___ 45. I need to overcome a "bad habit."

___ 46. I have looked at pornography on the computer in the past month.

___ 47. I have more than 5 drinks on average each week.

___ 48. I watch more than 2 hours of TV per day.

___ 49. I am on the internet more than 2 hours per day.

___ 50. I would be embarrassed if someone found out about certain websites I look at.

___ 51. I have bought a lottery ticket in the past month.

___ 52. I often try to find something that will give me a feeling of "thrill" or an adrenaline rush.

___ 53. My gambling has harmed my relationships in the past.

___ 54. Sometimes I go shopping to cope with stress.

___ 55. I eat too much or stop eating when I feel overwhelmed or anxious.

___ 56. When I am stressed I end up spending way too much or checks begin to bounce.

___ 57. I get a headache if I don't drink coffee or caffeinated drinks.

___ 58. My social life involves hanging out at bars or clubs.

___ 59. I have used marijuana or an illegal drug in the past 6 months.

___ 60. I have tried and failed to stop a bad habit.

**Past:**

___ 61. I have experienced trauma or loss in my life.

___ 62. I have been hit, punched, kicked or otherwise hurt by someone in my life.

___ 63. I did not have a happy childhood.

___ 64. I have complicated relationships with my parents.

___ 65. I do not feel loved by important people in my life.

___ 66. I am sometimes angry about my past.

___ 67. My past makes me question God's existence sometimes.

___ 68. I have been molested or sexually abused.

___ 69. I have major regrets about things I've

done in life.

___ 70. I often feel guilty about past mistakes I've made.

___ 71. I sometimes have flashbacks or memories of the past that make me feel anxious.

___ 72. I have been in jail.

___ 73. I have been part of a gang or cult.

___ 74. My parents had no idea what they were doing when raising me.

___ 75. It would be easier if I never had to speak to my parents or siblings again.

___ 76. I tend to not trust others because of my past.

___ 77. There are still consequences I am facing in my life because of my past decisions.

___ 78. I have had an abortion.

___ 79. I should have been dead by now because of risky things I've done.

___ 80. I feel haunted by my past and struggle to accept it for what it is.

### Self-care:

___ 81. I am not able to consistently exercise at least 3 times per week.

___ 82. I do not understand nutrition.

___ 83. I eat junk food (donuts, candy bars, chips, soda) at least once every day.

___ 84. I go to bed at different times each night.

___ 85. I do not have a bedtime routine.

___ 86. I wake up at different times every day or have swing-shifts at work.

___ 87. I get less than 7 hours of sleep per night.

___ 88. I have trouble falling asleep or staying asleep.

___ 89. I struggle to stick to a budget.

___ 90. A few of my bills are behind or I have more than $5000 in credit card debt.

___ 91. I do not have a hobby that I enjoy at least weekly.

___ 92. I have difficulty sitting quietly by myself.

___ 93. I struggle to manage stress well.

___ 94. It sometimes feels like a chore to get up and shower or get dressed.

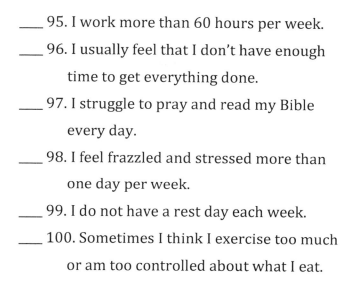

___ 95. I work more than 60 hours per week.

___ 96. I usually feel that I don't have enough time to get everything done.

___ 97. I struggle to pray and read my Bible every day.

___ 98. I feel frazzled and stressed more than one day per week.

___ 99. I do not have a rest day each week.

___ 100. Sometimes I think I exercise too much or am too controlled about what I eat.


When you have finished, look at each of the five sections. If you have five or more items checked in a particular area, it may point to an emotional trap. Consider talking to a counselor or pastor about ways in which you feel emotionally stuck. If you checked off question #7 and you currently feel unsafe, please seek immediate help at an emergency room.

# ABOUT THE AUTHOR

Kristen Kansiewicz is the founder and director of New Hope Christian Counseling, established in 2005 as a service of East Coast International Church in Lynn, MA. She graduated with a Bachelor of Arts degree in Psychology from Wheaton College (IL) and a Master of Arts in Counseling from Gordon Conwell Theological Seminary. She has established the Church Therapy Model, integrating professional counseling services into the church setting. Kristen is also a published author, regularly contributing to *Wyn Magazine* (www.wynmag.com) as well as *Children's Ministry Magazine* from Group Publishing.

Kristen's blog can be found at www.churchtherapy.com

Made in the USA
Middletown, DE
16 June 2016